D0566246

3 x ³/99 LT 5/96
/03 7X LT 10/02
  93 X 9 X 03
12/11 10X LT 12/05
10 x 1/16 LT 12/05

MODERN BOMBERS and ATTACK PLANES

MILITARY AIRCRAFT

MODERN BOMBERS and ATTACK PLANES

George Sullivan

 Facts On File

New York • Oxford

MODERN BOMBERS and ATTACK PLANES

Copyright © 1992 by George Sullivan

Facts On File, Inc.
460 Park Avenue South
New York NY 10016
USA

Facts On File Limited
c/o Roundhouse Publishing Ltd.
P.O. Box 140
Oxford OX2 7SF
United Kingdom

Library of Congress Cataloging-in-Publication Data
Sullivan, George.
    Modern bombers and attack planes / George Sullivan.
      p. cm. — (Military aircraft)
    Includes index.
    ISBN 0-8160-2354-9 (alk. paper)
    1. Attack planes. 2. Bombers. I. Title. II. Series.
    UG1242.A28S83 1992
    358.4′282—dc20   92–6399

A British CIP catalogue record for this book is available from the British Library.

Facts On File books are available at special discounts when purchased in bulk quantities for businesses, associations, institutions or sales promotions. Please contact our Special Sales Department in New York at 212/683-2244 (dial 800/322- 8755 except in NY, AK or HI) or in Oxford at 865/728399.

Text and jacket design by Ron Monteleone
Composition by Facts On File, Inc.
Manufactured by R.R. Donnelley & Sons, Inc.
Printed in the United States of America

Front cover photo: A B-2 bomber, courtesy of "USAF Photo via Northrop Corp."

10 9 8 7 6 5 4 3 2 1

This book is printed on acid-free paper.

CONTENTS

ACKNOWLEDGMENTS

Many individuals contributed information and photographs for use in this book. Special thanks are due the following: Bettie Sprigg, Department of Defense; Russell D. Egnor, Department of the Navy; Larry Wilson, Dan Hagadorne and Tim Cronin, National Air and Space Museum; Linda Dozell, North American Aircraft; Fred Polis, Boeing Military Airplanes; C. John Amrhein, Northrop Corporation; Barbara Hartnett, British Aerospace, Inc.; Sgt. Annette L. Snyder, Grand Forks Air Force Base, North Dakota; Capt. Louann J. Woods, McConnell Air Force Base, Kansas; and Francesca Kurti, TLC Labs.

INTRODUCTION

Bombers are platforms for launching weapons of different kinds. They date to the early years of World War I, which began in 1914 and was fought mainly in Europe.

The first bombers were small, rickety, single-engine, single-wing planes. The bombs were sometimes carried in a cloth sack in the cockpit. Once aloft over enemy territory, the pilot hurled them over the side one by one. Later, a mechanical device was developed that enabled the pilot to release the bombs from beneath the fuselage.

After World War I, aviation developed quickly. Many military leaders, however, were slow to realize the airplane's importance as a military weapon. One exception was General Billy Mitchell of the U.S. Army. He demonstrated the important role an airplane could play by bombing and sinking a retired German battleship.

During World War II, American and British bombers smashed Hitler's "Fortress Europe." Bombers also helped to hasten the defeat of Japan.

World War II saw the first all-metal bomber. And after the war, jet-powered bombers became standard in most of the world's best air forces. Propeller aircraft were seldom seen.

Today's bombers are of several different types. Some such as the B-52 Stratofortress, are big and awesome. Others, such as the Mirage IV or Panavia Tornado, are smaller and very quick.

The weapons today's bombers deliver cover a wide range. They can be conventional bombs or nuclear bombs. They can be long-range cruise missiles or short-range attack missiles. A plane on anti-submarine patrol might carry depth charges or mines.

The early bombing planes no more resemble today's bombers than the early Model-T Ford resembles a lightning-fast Indy racer or a big, stretch limousine. Yet the bomber's main role—dropping explosives on designated targets from the air—has not changed at all over the years. It's simply a matter of degree.

1 BOEING B-52 STRATOFORTRESS

"High-tech" isn't everything. During the war in the Persian Gulf, the headlines often went to the Stealth planes and "smart" bombs, to expensive wonder weapons. Yet the workhorse of the war was an airplane that began rolling off production lines in 1951, when Harry Truman was president and the United States was fighting the Korean War.

Built to travel 10,000 miles between refuelings, more than 50 B-52 Stratofortresses attacked Iraqi targets from bases as far away as Turkey, Great Britain and Spain, as well as from airfields in western parts of Saudi Arabia and from Diego Garcia, an island in the Indian Ocean about 3,000 miles south of the Persian Gulf. On each run, each B-52 dropped about 15 tons of explosives from 30,000 feet.

B-52s unloaded more bombs on Iraqi targets than any other aircraft operated by the allies. "There is no other weapon in our inventory with

The B-52G had the ability to deliver Hound Dog air-to-air missiles, one under each wing. (The Boeing Company)

B-52G FACT SHEET

Contractor: Boeing Military Airplanes

Type: Eight-engine long-range strategic bomber

Engines: Eight Pratt and Whitney J57-P-43WB turbojets, each delivering 13,750 lb. of thrust

Crew: Two pilots side by side, navigator, radar navigator, electronic warfare officer and fire control system operator (gunner)

Length: 160 ft., 10.9 in.

Height: 40 ft., 8 in.

Wingspan: 185 ft.

Loaded Weight: 488,000 lb.

Performance:

    Maximum Speed: 595 mph

    Service Ceiling: 60,000 ft.

    Range: 10,000 miles

First Flight: 1952

---

the capability to drop a lot of bombs and fly great distances," said Air Force Colonel David Young, who commanded the B-52 operation during the war. Rebuilt, re-winged, and re-engined at least a half dozen times since the 1960s, the B-52 demonstrated in the Persian Gulf that it had gotten better with age.

The B-52 is enormous—160 feet long with a 185-foot wingspan. It stretches five stories from the ground to the flight deck. It's takeoff weight is 488,000 pounds. The wing tips flex up and down as much as 17 feet when the plane is in flight.

About three-fourths of the B-52 is filled with fuel. "It's basically a flying gas tank," says one Air Force official.

The B-52G, originally meant for long-range bombing missions over the Soviet Union, has a flight range of 10,000 miles. The more modern B-52H, in service since 1961, has an 8,800-mile range. With midair refueling, the bombers can stay aloft indefinitely.

Most of the B-52s assigned to the Persian Gulf carried payloads of 51 bombs, each weighing 500 pounds. Although the B-52 was built to deliver nuclear weapons, the aircraft carried only conventional bombs during Operation Desert Storm.

The B-52, known in the Air Force as the BUFF—big, ugly, fat fellow—doesn't travel very fast, only about 500 miles per hour. Nor does it have a very staunch defensive system. The B-52G has 50-caliber guns in the tail turret. The H model is fitted out with a 20-mm cannon to ward off aircraft attacking from the rear.

Plans for the production of the B-52 date all the way back to 1945. World War II had just ended, and the United States, as the leader of the victorious Allies, had come to look upon itself as a global peacemaker, as a country with the mission of settling any disputes that might flare up among rival nations. To help fulfill this role, the U.S. Air Force realized that a long-range bomber was a necessity.

Boeing was given the contract for planning and designing the new aircraft. Two experimental B-52s, as the plane was named, were ordered by the Air Force. It took four years to develop the first prototype, which rolled off the Boeing production line on November 29, 1951.

That aircraft had most of the features of the models being flown today, including eight Pratt and Whitney turbojets carried in four pods under the giant wings, four twin-wheel landing trucks and a pressurized nose compartment for the crew. The plane had a massive fuel capacity in both the wings and fuselage.

The first production model of the aircraft, the B-52A, made its initial flight on August 5, 1954. Only three B-52As were built. All were used for testing and development.

In the years that followed, Boeing produced B-52s for the Air Force on a regular basis, with output reaching 20 a month in the late 1950s. Each successive model introduced new features.

In 1956, the Air Force demonstrated what the aircraft could accomplish, assigning eight B-52s to make nonstop flights over the North Pole that covered up to 17,000 miles. One plane, thanks to refueling, was in the air for 31½ hours. The following year, 1957, three B-52s flew around the world in 45 hours, 19 minutes, averaging 530 miles per hour.

The B-52G, which made its first flight on October 26, 1958, was the first of the B-52s to present important external changes. The nose had been slightly lengthened and the vertical fin was shortened. There were other major changes, including a boost in the plane's fuel capacity by some 46,000 gallons. In a change in the armament system, the gunner was moved from the tail to a position in the nose with the rest of the crew. The Air Force took delivery of the first of 193 B-52Gs on February 13, 1959.

The Air Force never grew tired of demonstrating the long-range capabilities of the B-52, and in August 1959 it sent a B-52G on a flight over every state capital in the continental United States, including Juneau, Alaska. The 12,942-mile nonstop flight took 21 hours.

The first B-52H, the last of the B-52 models, came off the Boeing production line on September 30, 1960 and made its first flight on March 6, 1961. Major changes included more powerful engines and the replacement of the aircraft's 50-caliber machine guns with a single Vulcan 20-mm cannon. Of the total of 744 aircraft that were produced, 102 were B-52Hs.

Through the years, the B-52 was continually upgraded to improve its navigation and the accuracy of its bomb delivery. Quick starters were added to the engines so they would all start at the same time. New

Tucked beneath the massive wing of an Air Force B-52, a bullet-shaped X-15, the first plane to break the sound barrier, is hardly visible. (North American Aviation)

underwing pylons enabled the plane to carry short- range attack missiles. These transformed the B-52 from an aircraft that could merely drop bombs to a "stand-off" bomber, one that could fire at its designated target from a distance as well.

Other improvements included forward-looking infrared (FLIR) and low-light-level TV sensors. These enabled the B-52 to fly at low levels so that it could evade the Soviet Union's air defenses. Stronger wings and a reinforced fuselage were also necessary to absorb the shock of flying so low. By the time the Persian Gulf War began, some B-52s also had an advanced navigation system that used information beamed by orbiting satellites.

Because of all the upgrading and improvements, some observers say the B-52s flying today are no longer the same planes. "It would surprise me if you found an original bolt in any one of them," said Early Tilford, Jr., a professor at the U.S. Air Force Air Command and Staff College.

Despite all the updating, the B-52 is no picnic to fly. Of its six man crew, only the pilot and the copilot, who are seated side by side, get to look out a window. An electronic-warfare officer and a fire control system operator—or, simply, a gunner—share tight quarters, quarters facing backward on the upper deck. The navigator and the radar navigator are seated below in a windowless space crammed with electronic gear.

Although these crews fly very long and difficult missions, some of which last longer than 24 hours, there's no room to stretch out for a nap. The roar from the eight jet engines is so loud that crew members can only talk to one another through headsets. The in-flight plumbing facilities are from an earlier era. Crew members discourage one another from going to the bathroom.

Beginning in 1955, B-52s served the nation as nuclear sentinels, ready to launch an attack at a moment's notice. Loaded with nuclear bombs, B-52s flew continuously above the United States so as not to be caught on the ground during a surprise attack by the nation's Cold War foe, the Soviet Union.

Those flights ended in 1968, but the tension between the two countries didn't. The flights were replaced by a ground alert force of B-52s, still loaded with nuclear bombs and ready to take to the air in an instant.

That state of readiness continued until 1991. In September of that year, President George Bush, recognizing what he called a "new world order," called for a large-scale cut in American nuclear weapons. Following the president's announcement, Defense Secretary Richard Cheney issued orders stating that "United States strategic bombers should stand down from their alert postures and their nuclear weapons shall be removed and stored in secure areas." Secretary Cheney's order affected 250 B-52s at 11 Air Force bases.

"This process can be reversed if need be," Secretary Cheney added. "It would take something less than 24 hours to restore the bombers to their former alert status."

The B-52 played a very active role in the Vietnam War, the longest of all the wars in which the United States has taken part. It began in 1957 and did not end until 1975.

At the time the United States became involved in Vietnam, the country was divided into North Vietnam, under the control of the Communists, and non-Communist South Vietnam. North Vietnamese troops and Communist-trained rebels, called the Viet Cong, fought to take over South Vietnam. The U.S. and South Vietnamese forces, helped by allies, sought to stop the North Vietnamese—but failed.

B-52s were used in Vietnam for more than eight years, from June 1965 to August 1973. They served as kind of a flying artillery, battering enemy supply lines, supply storage areas and troop concentrations.

This is a B-52H, the eighth and last model of the Stratofortress series. Delivery of the last B-52H occurred in October 1962. (The Boeing Company)

During the war, B-52s flew 126,615 missions. Some 55 percent were flown against targets in South Vietnam, 39 percent in Cambodia and Laos, where the North Vietnamese took sanctuary, and 6 percent in North Vietnam. In total, the Air Force lost 29 B-52s, 17 to enemy fire.

B-52s operated out of Anderson Air Force Base on Guam, an island in the Marianas Group some 2,250 miles from Vietnam. They were also based at U-Tapao in Thailand. B-52s flying sorties out of Anderson to Vietnam required refueling aloft from KC-135 tankers. No refueling was necessary on sorties flown from Thailand.

Since the primary mission of the B-52 had been to carry nuclear weapons, the aircraft had to be modified to handle so-called iron bombs. Known as the Big Belly modification, the work served to almost triple the planes internal bombload, increasing it from 22,000 pounds to 60,000 pounds. No changes were made outside of the aircraft. The wing pylons could still carry 24 bombs, each weighing 500 or 750 pounds.

B-52s went into action in Vietnam for the first time on June 18, 1965, when 27 of the planes made the long and difficult flight from Anderson Air Force Base on Guam, striking an enemy base in Binh Duong province north of Saigon. The raid was not a great success.

General William Westmoreland, who commanded U.S. forces in Vietnam between 1964 and 1968, considered the B-52 to be so vital in the conduct of the war that he dealt personally with requests for B-52 strikes from field commanders. Westmoreland himself also reviewed the targets and made the bomber assignments on a daily basis.

During 1965, B-52s flew 300 sorties a month. The number increased to 800 sorties a month during 1967. During February 1968, after the famous Tet offensive, the number got as high as 1,200 sorties.

Beginning in 1966, B-52s began to use what was called the "Combat Skyspot" bombing technique. Ground radar units directed the bombers to the target, then indicated the exact moment the bombs were to be released.

B-52s dumped millions of tons of bombs on a variety of targets. Time after time, they struck the Ho Chi Minh trail in Laos, over which the North Vietnamese funneled reinforcements and their battlefield supplies. They hit enemy troop concentrations in Cambodia.

During the long and bloody siege of the U.S. Marines at Khe Sanh from January through March 1968, the B-52s operated on an around-the-clock basis, with a three-plane B-52 "cell" arriving every 90 minutes. The North Vietnamese suffered heavy losses as a result of the constant punishment.

To the North Vietnamese soldiers, the B-52 was an instrument of terror. Being caught in a raid was like being struck by lightning. The bomb blasts shattered eardrums and sucked the air out of victims' lungs.

But the North Vietnamese soldiers learned to cope with the attacks by spreading out and holing up in deep bunkers. In that way, they managed to survive the raids.

In March 1972, North Vietnam launched a major invasion of South Vietnam. The United States answered back with some of the heaviest air strikes of the war against North Vietnam. Operation Linebacker, as the strikes were called by the U.S. command, inflicted heavy casualties on the North Vietnamese. It helped to halt the invasion and led to the opening of peace negotiations. As a show of good faith, the United States halted the bombing raids over 90 percent of North Vietnam's territory.

Henry A. Kissinger, President Nixon's national security adviser, represented the United States during peace negotiations, which were held in Paris. Le Duc Tho was the North Vietnamese representative. On October 26, the two announced they had come to an agreement on a peace plan. The United States said it would withdraw its forces from South Vietnam. North Vietnam agreed to return all American prisoners within 60 days. "We believe peace is at hand," Kissinger said.

But Kissinger was wrong. Complications ensued, and a final agreement could not be reached. President Nixon, when told by Kissinger what had taken place, gave the order "Execute Linebacker II."

Operation Linebacker II called for a massive attack by B-52s against North Vietnamese targets in the Hanoi-Haiphong area that had previously been "off limits." Except for a 24-hour Christmas break, the bombing lasted 11 days.

Targets included rail yards, power plants, communications facilities, radar installations, docks and shipping facilities, and ammunition storage areas. The bombers also hit airfields where MiG fighters were based.

The North Vietnamese responded by unleashing their entire supply of almost 1,000 surface-to-air missiles and a frightening barrage of antiaircraft fire. Fifteen B-52s were shot down and three damaged.

As his B-52 approached its target, Airman First Class Albert Moore, an 18-year-old tail gunner, called out SAM sightings over the plane's intercom system. "Pilot! SAM!," he said. "Twelve o'clock! Coming this way!" There were some near misses but the plane managed to avoid being hit.

Suddenly, Moore saw an unfamiliar blip on the radar screen—a MiG-21. As the small-tailed, delta-wing aircraft swung in behind and slightly to the left of the bomber, Moore called out a warning to the

A B-52 releases practice mines into Chin Hae Harbor, south of Pusan, during routine exercise with Republic of Korea forces. (U.S. Air Force)

other crew members. But there was little they could do because they were preparing for their bombing run, which was only a few seconds away.

Closing rapidly, the MiG dropped into a firing position behind the B-52. Moore locked into the enemy plane with his radar and opened fire with four 50-caliber machine guns. The B-52 shuddered with the first burst of gunfire. Moore's heart sank when he saw he had missed. He relaxed his grip, then fired again—and missed. Now the MiG was within 12,000 yards. Moore fired a third time, then breathed a sigh of relief as he saw the MiG's radar image suddenly explode and disappear from the screen.

At first, Moore couldn't believe what he had done. He had fired 800 rounds of ammunition and downed an enemy jet fighter. Later, back on the ground, Technical Sergeant Larry Chute, a gunner on another B-52, said he saw the plane Moore was shooting at burst into flame and pieces start to fall away. Moore's coolness and marksmanship earned him a Silver Star.

Although MiGs loomed as a severe threat, they were kept in check by fighter planes assigned to escort the B-52—and by the tail gunners. Surface-to-air-missiles were a far greater hazard.

On the first day of Linebacker II, more than 200 SAMs were launched at the attacking B-52s. Three aircraft were lost and two others damaged.

Day by day, Air Force planners changed B-52 tactics so as to reduce the effectiveness of the SAMs. The length of time over the target was cut from 30 minutes to 15 minutes. The flight pattern the planes were flying was adjusted to get the B-52s over the water faster, following their bombing runs. More electronic equipment was added to jam SAM radar and prevent accurate targeting.

Captain John Mize, on his fourth mission of Linebacker II, was executing a steep turn away from the target area when a SAM blasted into his plane's left wing. The huge plane shook crazily and warning lights started flashing in the cockpit. All four port engines were knocked out and one was afire. The plane began to fall like a stone. Before Mize could get the wounded aircraft to level off, several thousand feet of altitude had been lost.

Most members of the six-man crew had suffered shrapnel injuries when the SAM exploded. Only a handful of flight systems were working. Mize had no radar, no computers. But he did have a radio, altimeter and air speed indicator.

Not only was the plane almost helpless, it had lost the protection of other aircraft. Two more SAMs were fired toward the plane but they both missed. Fortunately, no MiGs spotted the wounded bird.

Before long, the flaming engine burned itself out. Mize and the other crew members began trying to coax their plane toward friendly territory.

Because the only engines operating were the four in the right wing, the B-52 kept losing altitude. Mize's goal was to try to get the plane at least as far as the Thailand border. Once over Thailand, it would be safe to bail out.

As they got closer to the border, more trouble developed. The bomb bay doors suddenly flew open and one of the plane's landing gear started cycling up and down. These weird happenings added to the tension.

Despite the problems, the plane kept making headway and eventually crossed the border. For a time, Mize thought they might even be able to make a safe landing at Nakhon Phanom air base in Thailand, but the crew couldn't manage to keep the plane airborne. Mize had no choice but to give the order to eject. All the ejection seats worked, except the navigator's. He made his exit through an escape hatch.

View from a tanker plane during a B-52 refueling operation. (The Boeing Company)

At the time the crew members ejected, their plane was only eight miles from Nakhon Phanom, and all were rescued. Captain Mize received the Air Force Cross for his heroic efforts. Other members of the crew were awarded the Distinguished Flying Cross. All received Purple Hearts, too.

As the B-52s continued to pound enemy defenses, SAMs became less of a problem. They were seldom seen by the end of the Linebacker II campaign.

The bombing ended on December 29. Immediately after, the two sides were back at the negotiating table. A cease-fire agreement was signed on January 27, 1973. It provided for the withdrawal of all U.S. and allied forces and the return of all prisoners.

During Linebacker II, the Air Force dropped an amount of explosives that was about equal to that of the nuclear bomb used at Hiroshima at the end of World War II. It was however, spread out over 729 sorties against 34 different targets.

Air Force supporters hail Linebacker II as a great triumph. They look upon it as a club that forced the North Vietnamese to sit down at the bargaining table and eventually sign a peace treaty.

They go further. Some say that Linebacker II provides evidence that the United States could have won the war if the nation had the will to hit the North Vietnamese with huge quantities of bombs sooner.

But other military experts point out that the heavy and constant bombing did not have any great effect on widely scattered dug-in troops. And what losses the enemy did suffer were replaced with new troops. Supplies and equipment lost to bombing were replaced with fresh stores from China and the Soviet Union. Bombing or not, the North Vietnamese never lost the willingness or ability to fight.

In 1974, North Vietnamese troops went back on the attack. The war ended when South Vietnam surrendered to North Vietnam on April 30, 1975.

To some people, the B-52 is associated with nuclear weapons, and only nuclear weapons. It is true that at one time most B-52s were armed with nuclear bombs to deter a feared attack by the Soviet Union.

The first nuclear bombs were huge, weighing as much as four or five tons. The first hydrogen bombs were even larger.

The B-52 was designed to carry a single nuclear bomb with a diameter of 8 feet and a length of 25 feet, somewhat the same size as a chauffeured limousine.

During the 1950s, while the explosive power of nuclear bombs multiplied, their size and weight were reduced. One free-fall nuclear bomb, turned out in large quantities, was designated the B28. It weighed 5,500 pounds and was carried by the B-52 in groups of four.

In January 1966, two B28 bombs fell into the Mediterranean Sea off the coast of Spain after a B-52 collided in midair with a tanker. The bombs were ripped apart and released some radioactive material. But thanks to the complex arming system of the bombs, there was no thermonuclear explosion. During the 1980s, the U.S. Air Force had close to 1,000 B28s in its inventory.

Missiles went through the same stages of development as nuclear bombs. The first were noted for their massive size and weight. Today's missiles are so much smaller that a great many can be carried inside a bomber's weapons bays.

The first air-to-ground missile to be carried by the B-52 was the AGM-28 Hound Dog, which dates to 1959. The lanky Hound Dog, some 45 feet long, was as tall as a telephone pole. Two of them were carried under the inner wings of the B-52. Each Hound Dog weighed almost 5 tons.

To assist the B-52 in taking off, the engines of the two missiles were started and run up to full thrust. Once the B-52 was airborne, the missile engines were shut down until the weapons were ready for release. The Air Force retired the Hound Dog in 1976.

In the years before the war in the Persian Gulf, some B-52s were armed with short-range attack missiles, SRAMs. A B-52 can carry 20 SRAMs—eight internally and six under each wing. Each SRAM has a range of 100 miles.

SRAMs were succeeded by air-launched cruise missiles, ALCMs, each with a range of 1,500 miles. The B-52 can carry 12 ALCMs, six under each wing. At first, ALCMs were installed on the B-52G only, but during the mid-1980s the B-52H was refitted to carry them also.

Bombs have become high-tech, too. There are "smart" bombs, for instance. Smart bombs are guided bombs. They have control systems that direct them to the target. In other words, they use the same targeting techniques as guided missiles. Not only are smart bombs much more

In Air Force circles, B-52 is sometimes referred to as the BUFF—big, ugly, fat fellow. (The Boeing Company)

accurate than free-fall bombs, they enable an aircraft to remain some distance from the target and the antiaircraft fire that's likely to surround it.

Free-fall bombs, also called gravity bombs, unguided missiles or iron bombs, come in many different sizes, weighing from a few pounds to over a ton. There are several different types. Cluster bomb units (CBUs) are containers of small bombs. When the container is dropped, it breaks open in midair and spreads the bomblets over a wide area. A typical 600-pound CBU contains 150 smaller bombs, each weighing about 3 pounds.

CBUs carry a variety of loads—incendiary, antitank and chemical. In addition, the bombs can be equipped with timers or sensors, which, in effect, transform the bombs into land mines.

Incendiaries are bombs that ignite upon bursting. They are also referred to as napalm bombs, napalm being a highly flammable jellylike substance, sort of a thickened gasoline.

In recent years, ordinary incendiary bombs have been replaced by fuel air explosives (FAE). When an FAE smacks into the ground, it breaks open and sends up a big cloud of flammable mist. A small delayed action explosive then goes off, causing the cloud to burst into flame. It's not merely the heat and flames that do the damage. The pressure generated by the explosion wrecks vehicles and tanks, destroys supplies and equipment and can be fatal to any personnel in the area.

Because of their ability to wreak destruction over a wide area, FAE bombs are effective in clearing land mines. In Vietnam they were used to create helicopter landing sites in the thickest of jungles.

The air campaign in the Persian Gulf was run from several basement offices in the headquarters of the Royal Saudi Air Force that had been turned over to the U.S. Air Force. There Lieutenant General Charles (Chuck) Horner, who commanded the allied air forces during the Gulf war, Brigadier General Buster C. Glosson, and dozens of other officers figured out what their targets were to be each day and what weapons or delivery systems were best suited to destroy them.

President George Bush had set the overall objective: Force Saddam Hussein out of Kuwait. At the same time, the allies wanted to eliminate the Iraqi army as a threat to the region and do away with the nation's ability to wage war with chemical and biological weapons.

In the months before January 1991, when the bombing began, Generals Horner and Glosson and their staff members established these priorities:

- Destroy Saddam Hussein's command-and-control network.

- Demolish his nuclear and chemical warfare facilities, radar, SAMs, antiaircraft missiles and air force.
- Destroy the factories and supply depots vital to the military.
- Destroy airfields and ports, highways and bridges.
- Cripple the fighting ability of his top troops, the Republican Army.

In the final phase of the air operation, planes would furnish support as the ground forces went into battle.

Besides their bombers and attack aircraft—chiefly the B-52s (the Big Uglies), A-10s (the Warthogs) and the F-16s (the Killer Bees)—General Horner and his staff had several different kinds of cruise missiles in their arsenal. These they planned to use on what they called "soft" targets, those not protected by thick walls of concrete. Soft targets included petroleum storage tanks and power stations. The planners timed the missiles so they would arrive before or after the bombing raids. In that way, Iraq would be under attack almost 24 hours a day.

The enormous size of the operation, with more than 2,000 sorties a day, required a vast amount of careful planning. Flight plans had to be

The B-52 has been rebuilt, re-winged and re-engined at least a half a dozen times. (The Boeing Company)

developed by computer just to keep all the airplanes from running into one another. A great fleet of aerial tankers had to be kept in the air on practically an around-the-clock basis so the bombers could refuel.

The air assault began on January 16, 1991 and continued without letup for 40 days and nights. The B-52s were successful in bombing Iraqi ammunition depots, warehouses and factories. They were less effective against dug-in Iraqi troops. Waves of B-52s were also used on targets on the outskirts of Baghdad. These targets often included electrical plants and oil facilities.

By the sixth or seventh day of the war, Iraq no longer had the ability to generate electricity. "Not one electron was flowing," said an Air Force officer.

The loss of Iraq's electrical power created a number of benefits for the allied forces. It weakened Iraqi air defenses and communications between commanders and their forces in the field.

Lieutenant General Charles A. Horner, who had overall command of the air campaign, said that knocking out the electricity had a psychological effect on the Iraq citizens that he called a "side benefit." Said General Horner: "The message is loud and clear that they are involved in a war and it is not going well."

So thorough was the destruction that nearly four months after the war, Iraq was able to produce only about 20 percent of the electricity that it had produced before the war. From the standpoint of electric power, Iraq had been bombed back to 1920.

The allies attacked Iraqi oil facilities with much the same degree of success. The targets included major storage tanks, pipelines and junctions, and terminals and refineries. Because of the bombing, Iraq's military was suffering an almost complete loss of "all motive power" by the end of the war.

Allied forces launched a major ground offensive against Iraq on February 24, 1991. The terrible battering that Iraqi troops had taken from the air had destroyed their will to fight. On March 3, the Iraqi military accepted all demands for a permanent cease-fire. The war was over.

Several times during its long history, the B-52 has had stiff competition from other bombers that have interested the U.S. Air Force planners. Yet the B-52 has always managed to survive.

During the early 1960s, the Air Force developed the B-70 Valkyrie, a manned bomber. It was said the plane would be able to travel at three times the speed of sound at an altitude of 70,000 feet. But at about the same time the B-70 was becoming operational, the Air Force figured out that the way for a plane to evade Soviet radar and antiaircraft fire was to fly lower, not higher. Who needed a plane that cruised at 70,000 feet? The B-70 was scrapped.

A decade later, Rockwell International worked with the Air Force to improve the B-1, which eventually became the B-1B. By the mid-1980s, Rockwell had produced 100 B-1Bs. But the plane was less than a success. Often it was grounded, for reasons ranging from fuel leaks to birds caught in the engines. None served in the Persian Gulf war.

During the early 1990s, the B-52 faced yet another challenge from the B-2 Stealth bomber. But B-2s, because they cost $865 million apiece and have never been tested in combat, face an uncertain future.

One thing the Persian Gulf war served to demonstrate is that some relatively inexpensive weapons can be more effective than most people thought. With continued improvements, the Air Force's fleet of B-52s is certain to serve the nation into the next century.

2 ROCKWELL B-1B LANCER

From the plane's beginnings in the late 1960s, the B-1B, a sleek and very powerful plane packed with sophisticated electronics, has been the subject of hot debate. To General Bernard Randolf, chief of the U.S. Air Force Systems Command, the B-1B is "the best warplane in the world." To others, however, it is unnecessary and unworkable, and *U.S. News and World Report* dubbed it "a flying lemon."

Officially named the Lancer in 1990, the B-1B is a four-engine, swing-wing bomber with the ability to penetrate enemy defenses either at low altitude and high subsonic speed or at high altitude and supersonic speed. It carries a crew of four and can deliver eight cruise missiles, 12 to 24 nuclear bombs or 40 tons of general purpose bombs.

The Persian Gulf war increased the controversy over the plane. During the 43-day bombing campaign, when B-52s and A-10s were earning high praise, little was heard of the B-1B. That's because the plane sat out the war.

The Air Force said that the B-1B was primarily a nuclear bomber (and the Persian Gulf war was a non-nuclear war). A spokesperson explained that the Air Force wanted to keep the B-1Bs at their bases in the United States in their traditional role of deterring a nuclear strike from the Soviet Union.

At the time, early 1991, the Air Force had 97 B-1Bs in operation. Approximately one-third of those planes were on what the Air Force calls "active alert."

Another and equally important reason why the B-1B spent the war on the sidelines was because the entire fleet was grounded at the time. On two occasions in the months before the war began, engines on B-1Bs had failed. The two aircraft had landed safely without injury to members of the crew. Nevertheless, the Air Force decided to ground all B-1Bs until the engine problem could be investigated and corrected.

The B-1B had a long and stormy development career. There were even times when it looked like the plane would never be built at all.

A B-1B from Ellsworth Air Force Base, South Dakota, photographed from the tanker following in-flight refueling. (U.S. Air Force)

B-1B FACT SHEET

Prime Contractor: Rockwell International

Type: Long-range strategic bomber and missile carrier

Engines: Four General Electric F101-GE-102 turbofans, each delivering 30,780 pounds of thrust

Crew: Basic crew of four: pilot, copilot and two systems operators (offensive and defensive)

Length: 147 ft.

Height: 34 ft.

Wingspan:

    Fully Spread: 136 ft., 8½ in.

    Fully Swept: 78 ft., 21½ in.

Loaded Weight: 477,000 lb.

Performance:

    Maximum Speed: 700–750 mph

    Service Ceiling: 60,000 ft.

    Range: 7,450 miles

First Flight: 1974

In December 1957, about 2½ years after the first B-52 Stratofortress had been delivered, the Air Force began developing a bomber that some day might be its successor. North American Aviation won the contract to produce the new plane, which was to be called the XB-70. The plane was going to be able to cruise at three times the speed of sound (about 2,000 miles an hour) at 70,000 feet.

But the B-70 program was canceled before a single production aircraft was built. On May 1, 1960, a Soviet radar-guided surface-to-air missile brought down an American U-2 spy plane over the city of Sverdlovsk. The pilot, Francis Gary Powers, managed to parachute to safety.

The incident heated up the cold war and was personally embarrassing to President Dwight D. Eisenhower. He put a stop to spy-plane flights over the Soviet Union, at least for a time.

To the U.S. Air Force, the shooting down of the U-2 was an eye-opener. The plane had been cruising at 70,000 feet and yet a Soviet missile had been able to pluck it out of the sky. The Air Force decided the XB-70 was not to be the bomber of the future. Something very different was needed.

Radar's weakest point is detection near the ground. The radio waves it sends out cannot go over or around obstacles presented by natural terrain in seeking to detect an object such as a low-flying aircraft. That fact led Air Force planners to the conclusion that the best way to be able to reach enemy targets of the future was to go in at a very low altitude and subsonic speed.

Other Air Force experts disagreed. They believed that bombers of the 1980s and 1990s were going to have to be able to fly at supersonic speed near the target area. The debate continued for years. It is why the B-1B was built. The most notable feature of the new aircraft was its "swing wings." Pivoting out from the fuselage, the wings could be spread to a length of 136 feet, 8½ inches for takeoffs, landings and low-speed flight. At high altitude when great speed was needed, the wings could be tucked back against the fuselage. This special feature is what makes the B-1B so tactically versatile.

The B-1B has four turbofan engines mounted in pairs under the rear of each of the wings. Another unique feature is the aircraft's SMCS

A B-1B towers over guests at roll-out ceremony at Palmdale, California in 1984. The plane was first flown in October 1984. (Rockwell International)

(structural model control system), designed to give stability to the plane when flying at low levels in turbulent air. The SMCS consists of sensors that register unwanted up-or-down or sideways movement of the aircraft, and then eliminate it by automatically adjusting the rudder or other control surfaces.

Late in December 1974, the B-1 made its first test flight. Early the next year, the plane flew supersonically for the first time. Congress then appropriated the money necessary to build the first production models of the aircraft. The B-1 was scheduled to enter service in mid-1979 as a nuclear armed strategic bomber capable of penetrating enemy defenses either at low altitude and high subsonic speeds or at high altitude and a high Mach.

But in June 1977, the B-1 ran into a roadblock. President Jimmy Carter canceled the B-1 program. "During the last few months, I have done my best to assess all of the factors involving the production of the B-1 bomber," Carter said at a press conference. "My decision is that we should not continue with deployment of the B-1, and I am directing that we discontinue plans for the production of the weapons system." Carter called it " . . . one of the most difficult decisions I have made since I have been in office."

Carter explained that one of the reasons he was canceling the B-1 was the successful development of long-range air-launched cruise missiles. These, along with the availability of the nation's fleet of B-52s, provided adequate defense for the nation, Carter said.

Carter was voted out of office in 1980 and Ronald Reagan became president. Reagan took a tough stance toward the Soviet Union, warning that the United States must keep strong militarily to assure lasting peace. He called for increased spending on missiles, submarines and bombers. In October 1981, as part of his call for a military buildup, President Reagan announced that his administration planned to order 100 B-1s.

The new plane, designated the B-1B, made its first flight on October 18, 1984. The biggest difference between the former plane, the B-1A, and the new version, the B-1B, was in weight. The B-1B was rated at 477,000 pounds, compared with 395,000 pounds for the original model. The increased weight was due chiefly to greater fuel capacity and the installation of heavy equipment for launching cruise missiles. Improved electronics had also been added to improve the plane's ability to penetrate enemy defenses.

Another modification involved reducing the aircraft's radar image, its radar cross section. This was achieved by streamlining certain external features and using more materials that can reflect radar waves.

The first production model of the plane was ready for delivery to the Air Force in September 1984. At that time, Rockwell was producing B-1Bs at the rate of one a month. But within two years, the production rate had jumped to one plane a week. The step-up in production enabled the company to turn out the 100th B-1B on January 20, 1988, several weeks ahead of schedule.

In 1987, the B-1B established a number of speed-distance-payload records. On July 4 of that year, a B-1B took off with a payload of 66,140 pounds. Flying a closed course near Vandenburg Air Force Base in California, the bomber covered 1,240 miles (2,000 kilometers) at an average speed of 669.96 miles an hour.

Even before the B-1B started rolling off the production line, the Air Force had picked out four bases to receive the new plane. They were Dyess Air Force Base near Abilene, Texas; Ellsworth Air Force Base, near Rapid City, South Dakota; Grand Forks Air Force Base, west of Grand Forks, North Dakota; and McConnell Air Force Base, southeast of Wichita, Kansas.

The first production model B-1Bs arrived at Dyess Air Force Base in June 1985. Dyess was eventually home to 29 B-1Bs.

Tim Cole, science/technology/aerospace editor for *Popular Mechanics* magazine, flew with the crew of a B-1B, taking off from Dyess Air Force Base to head for what the Air Force calls the Strategic Training Range Complex, a wide stretch of land that covers hundreds of miles of grasslands and rolling hills over the states of Wyoming, Colorado, South Dakota and Montana. The flight was a low-level bombing run against an imaginary enemy.

As the "attack" began, the plane flew at ground-hugging levels over the Wyoming countryside, seeking to outrun a phantom enemy fighter. The plane's Structural Mode Control System (SMCA) leveled out the bumps. Cole, harnessed to his seat, an oxygen mask over his helmet, found the ride surprisingly smooth. "I have no difficulty keeping the lemonade in my cup," he reported.

From time to time, the low-flying plane banked sharply around hillsides. The pilot and copilot discussed flight strategies meant to outwit enemy planes. "Let's duck behind that mountain." "Can you squeeze over that hill?" "How about down inside that canyon?" All the while, the offensive systems operator was bent over his radar screen keeping alert for quick changes in the terrain.

During the mission, the plane locked onto targets over Powell, Wyoming; Forsyth, Montana; and Belle Fourche, South Dakota. When the

The B-1B has many fighterlike qualities, including the ability to fly at supersonic speeds. Here the plane is escorted by an Air Force F-15. (Rockwell International)

bomb release button was pressed, a tone sounded. The accuracy of the "drop" was scored by a computer.

Cole quoted Colonel Don Jensen, a commander of the 96th Bombardment Wing stationed at Dyess, as saying, "We're incredibly accurate. We're so accurate it's like throwing an egg at 900 feet per second and hitting a trash can with it."

But while the B-1B could perform with perfection at times, the aircraft had more than its share of problems. On the morning of September 28, 1987, a B-1B took off from Dyess on a low-level training mission—and never returned. Flying fast and low near La Junta, Colorado, the plane collided with a bird the size of a pelican. According to one account of the incident, the crew heard a loud bang and then the aircraft began to shudder and make groaning sounds. The bird had been sucked into the plane's engines. Fuel and electrical lines snapped and fire broke out.

The pilot fought to get the plane higher to give the crew time to get out. Three crew members made it. But two observer/instructors and the pilot, who chose to stay at the controls to keep the plane in the air for as long as possible to give his friends a chance, went down with the aircraft, which was totally destroyed.

After the crash, the first to involve a production model B-1B, and the investigation that followed, the Air Force made some changes in the B-1B in an effort to prevent future bird strikes from dooming the big plane. Shields were installed to protect the fuel and hydraulic lines and electrical systems.

Leaking fuel tanks—called "seeps and weeps"—were another problem. They weren't big leaks but even small drips of leaking fuel are enough to keep a plane from flying. Several aircraft were grounded as a result of the leaks.

The B-1B is what is called a "wet wing" plane. That means the fuel is pumped directly into the wings, rather than into flexible bladders built into them. In each plane, 290,000 metal fasteners and five miles of metal-to-metal connections must be sealed to prevent seepage.

To find out what was wrong, Air Force mechanics put on protective clothing and crawled inside the fuel tanks. They found that in some of the first airplanes to come off the production line the pastelike material used to seal the connections had not been applied properly. Putting on new sealant seemed to solve the problem.

A much bigger problem concerned the B-1B's electronic countermeasures—or ECM—system, meant to enable the plane to evade enemy radar defenses. In the B-1B, radar-jamming gear reaches—or was supposed to reach—its highest state of development.

The B-1B's ECM system weighs almost three tons and consists of 107 interconnecting "black boxes" that are distributed throughout the plane. The system was designed to perform these tasks:

- Detect all enemy radar signals from the ground.
- Sort out the signals according to how threatening each seems to be, and respond by sending out false signals to those that are judged to be the most serious. (By responding only to a select number of signals, the system conserves power.)
- Display all of this information on a screen.
- Permit a human operator to override all decisions made by the ECM computer.

There were more than a few snags with the system. Well over a year after the first B-1Bs went into operation, the ECM receivers and transmitters were still being tinkered with. General Elbert Harbour, the program chief for the B-1B, told *Science* magazine that there were failings with the system's computer program, its software. It gave the system "all kinds of crazy instructions," General Harbour said. A final version of the ECM system, able to cope with the latest developments in Soviet radars, was not scheduled to be installed aboard the B-1B until the early 1990s.

In 1988, a second B-1B crashed. The plane was practicing landings at Dyess Air Force Base, when its engines suddenly caught fire. After the pilot ordered the crew members to bail out, he flew the plane away from residential areas before bailing out himself. The plane crashed and burned in a wooded area. While the Air Force has not been able to establish the exact cause of the fire, it has been determined that it was fed by a fuel leak.

Not long after, a third B-1B crashed while coming in for a landing at Ellsworth Air Force Base. On days when there are low-hanging clouds, pilots often try to get beneath the ceiling so they can see the runway when landing rather than rely wholly on instruments. In this case, the pilot went too low, and the aircraft pancaked into the runway.

Its wings spread, its landing gear down, a B-1B glides in for a landing at McConnell Air Force Base, Kansas. (McConnell Air Force Base)

All four members of the crew managed to escape injury, however, thanks to the pilot and the B-1B's ejection system. Each of the four crew members sat in an aluminum ejection seat. Beneath the seat were small explosive charges. As the plane slammed into the runway, the pilot pulled a handle that in a split second blew open the crewmen's hatches and rocketed each of them into the air. Each man was blasted high enough to make his parachute open automatically.

B-1B crashes and other problems that have led to groundings of the aircraft have provided ammunition to the plane's critics.

The Air Force and others who support the B-1B say the problems the plane has experienced are not untypical for a new aircraft. They point out the B-52 also experienced serious fuel leaks and that its first production model, the B-52B, of which 50 were built, had a very brief service life, lasting barely one full year. In the end, these "teething troubles," as they've been called, didn't prevent the B-52 from having a very long and distinguished career.

"History will tell us that this is one hell of a machine," General Elbert Harbour once told *Science* magazine, in speaking of the plane. "The trouble is," he added, "history is terribly slow in delivering messages."

3 TUPOLEV Tu-16 BADGER

In the Persian Gulf war in 1991, the U.S. Air Force demonstrated with the B-52 bomber that an aircraft well beyond the age of 30 can still play an important role in modern warfare. In the Tu-16 Badger, the Russians have evidence to support that argument. Developed during the early 1950s and first produced in quantity in 1954, the Tu-16 is still going strong.

The Tu-16 also has a future. Besides the many hundreds that are in use in what used to be called the Soviet Union, the aircraft is also in service with the Chinese Air Force. The plane continues to be produced in China, where it has been designated the Xian H-6.

First flown in the winter of 1951–52, the Tupolev Tu-16 Badger has remained in service to this day. (National Air & Space Museum)

Tu-16 FACT SHEET

Designer: Tupolev OKB

Type: Medium-range strategic bomber

Engines: Two Mikulin RD-3M turbojets, each delivering 20,950 lb. of thrust

Crew: Normal crew of six—two pilots side by side, two gunner/observers, one radio operator/gunner, one navigator/bombardier

Length: 118 ft., 11¼ in.

Height: 45 feet., 11¼ in.

Wingspan: 108 ft., 11¼ in.

Loaded Weight: 165,350 lb.

Performance:

   Maximum Speed: 616 mph

   Service Ceiling: 40,350 ft.

   Range: 2,485 miles

First Flight: Winter 1951–52

About 2,000 Tu-16s were produced by the Soviet Union. Several hundred of these are still in service.

At one time, according to the U.S. Air Force, about 200 Tu-16s were available for a strike role with the Soviet Air Force in Smolensk and Irkutsk. These aircraft were equipped to carry either nuclear or conventional weapons.

A number of Tu-16s were converted to use as tankers. This was accomplished by mounting a fuel tank in a plane's weapons bay and installing a hose system in the tip of the right wing. (The Badger uses an unusual wing tip to wing tip method of refueling. The aircraft to be refueled flies behind the tanker. A hose is trailed from the tanker's right wing tip to the receiving plane's left wing tip.) Approximately 20 Tu-16 tankers have been assigned to support the bombers based in Smolensk and Irkutsk.

These planes were also aided by about 155 other Tu-16s that were equipped for reconnaissance and electronic countermeasures (ECM) duties.

In addition, Soviet Naval Aviation flew the Tu-16. It had about 100 attack aircraft operating from shore bases plus as many as 70 tankers and some 80 reconnaissance and ECM aircraft.

Soviet Tu-16s were active for many years over the Atlantic Ocean, North Sea, Baltic Sea, Black Sea and in the Far East. About a dozen were stationed at Cam Ranh Bay in Vietnam, the huge base built during the Vietnam War by U.S. forces. Not only strike aircraft, but tankers and ECM planes were based there.

The name *Tu-16 Badger* comes from several sources. The Tu refers to Andrei Tupolev, who, before his death in 1972, was the leading designer of Soviet multi-engine bombers. Born in 1888, Tupolev designed what has been called the best Soviet bomber of World War II, the Tu-2.

A special design bureau bearing Tupolev's name was founded in 1929. His son, Dr. Alexei A. Tupolev, was one of the bureau's chief designers.

The Tupolev Design Bureau was one of several that served the military complex of what was once the Soviet Union. They were known as OKBs, which stands for Opytno-Konstruktorskoye Byuro, meaning Experimental Construction Bureau. Of all the OKBs, the Mikoyan/Gurevich—or MiG—OKB was the best known. It designed the famous MiG fighters.

As for the Badger's numerical designation, 16, that came from the fact that all Soviet air military aircraft were identified in sequence of development by two-digit numbers. Even numbers went to multi-engine bombers and transport planes. Odd numbers were assigned to fighters.

The name *Badger* did not come from the Soviets. It was assigned to the aircraft by the Air Standards Coordinating Committee of the North Atlantic Treaty Organization (NATO).

During the cold war, when there were often periods of tension and even military confrontation between the Soviet Union and the United States and its Western European allies, the Soviets seldom gave out any information about their aircraft. They wouldn't even disclose how they were to be designated.

So NATO devised its own system. Names were used that would be easily understandable when the planes were being referred to during radio communication, even when there were periods of poor reception.

Each name imparted the basic mission of the aircraft. Names beginning with B were bombers. Not only did the Soviets have the Badger, but also the Backfire, Blinder, Blackjack and Bear.

F stood for fighters. Flogger, Foxbat, Fulcrum and Foxhound were some of them.

About 2,000 Badgers have been built in a dozen different versions. (National Air & Space Museum)

Single-syllable names indicated a propeller driven aircraft, while multisyllable names were used to designate jets.

The Tu-16 Badger's name indicates it is a jet-powered bomber.

NATO also designated variations of the original model with letters. The second Tu-16 to be identified became the Tu-16 Badger-B, the third, the Badger-C, etc.

Not only was the Tu-16 Badger hailed for its long life, it also won praise for the many different roles it played. The different versions were as follows:

Badger-A—The basic twin-engine jet bomber, able to carry nuclear or conventional weapons. It was fitted with three gun turrets—ventral (in the plane's belly), dorsal (on its back) and tail. Each turret was armed with two 23-mm cannons. A seventh cannon was mounted in the nose to be fired by the pilot. Some of these were fitted to serve as flight refueling tankers.

Badger-C—An antishipping aircraft first seen in 1961 during Soviet Aviation Day maneuvers, the Badger-C carried a big air-to-surface missile—termed Kipper by NATO—under its fuselage. The aircraft also had a radome—radar housing—in its nose in place of the cannon in Badger-A.

Badger-D—An electronic reconnaissance version of the Tu-16, the job of the Badger-D was to pinpoint sea-going targets for missile launch crews aboard ships and also for strike aircraft too distant from the target for precise missile aiming. The Badger-D had a large under-nose radome, plus three smaller radomes arranged one behind the other under the weapons bay.

Badger-E—Used for both photographic and electronic reconnaissance, the Badger-E was similar to the Badger-A, but with camera windows in the doors of the weapons bay. There were also two additional radomes under the fuselage.

Badger-F—While very similar to the Badger-E, the Badger-F had an electronics intelligence pod under each wing. There was no radome beneath the fuselage.

Badger-G—Converted from a Badger-B, this version served chiefly with antishipping squadrons of the Soviet Naval Air Force. The aircraft was fitted with underwing pylons for rocket-powered air-to-surface

A Tu-16 Badger attracts the attention of a pair of Navy carrier-based F-4 Phantoms. (National Air & Space Museum)

missiles, designated Kelt by NATO, that could be carried a distance of some 2,000 miles.

A modified version of the Badger-G, designed to carry the Kingfish air-to-surface missile, was first seen in 1981. It had a large radome beneath the fuselage to be used in locating missile targets.

A number of Badger-Gs were transferred to the Iraqi Air Force and saw combat duty during the Iran-Iraqi War, which broke out in 1980 and raged until a cease-fire was arranged in 1988. These planes conducted at least one bombing raid against the Tehran airport and several missile attacks against other Iranian targets.

Badger-H—An electronic countermeasure (ECM) aircraft, the Badger-H had as its primary role the dropping of chaff, which are long strips of aluminum foil intended to jam enemy radar and electronic communications. The Badger-H was capable of carrying 20,000 pounds of chaff. The chaff dispensers were located in the weapons bay. The plane was also fitted with a pair of teardrop radomes, one just in front of and the other behind the weapons bay.

Badger-J—Like the Badger-H, this was an ECM aircraft. But the Badger-J was fitted out with electronics-jamming equipment, some of which was housed in a canoe-shaped radome beneath the plane's belly. The aircraft was first identified in 1987.

A number of Badger-Js were based at Cam Ranh Bay in Vietnam, assigned to flying patrols over the South China Sea near the Philippines.

Badger-K—Used in electronic reconnaissance, the Badger-K was first identified in 1981. It was similar to the Badger-E, but had two teardrop-shaped radomes, one in front of and the other behind the weapons bay.

Badger-L—First identified during August 1986 in an article in the Soviet magazine *Aviation and Cosmonautics*, this was another ECM aircraft. It had an added radome at the end of the plane's nose and several smaller electronics blisters under the nose and along the sides of the fuselage.

The Chinese version of the Tu-16, built at Xian, has been designated the H-6. In May 1966, the aircraft was used by China to drop the nation's third nuclear bomb.

The first production models of the H-6 were delivered in 1968, approximately 10 years after the first Tu-16 had entered service in China. By 1987, it was estimated that the Chinese had produced about 120 H-6s. Most of these are bombers, but it is believed that there are also tanker, reconnaissance and ECM versions of the aircraft.

Beginning in the late 1950s, the Soviet Union began to equip its long-range bombers with small-winged air-to-surface missiles, ASMs.

The first, designated the Kennel by NATO, was enormous in size, weighing almost 6,600 pounds. It had a range of 90 miles.

Similar in shape to a swept-wing jet, the Kennel flew part of the way to the target on an autopilot system. When it got close, it used nose radar to help find its target.

The Tu-16 Badger-B carried a Kennel under each wing. In 1961, the Badger-C carried a much larger and faster missile. NATO dubbed it the Kipper. About 31 feet long, the belly-mounted Kipper was believed to be able to travel at supersonic speed. It had a range of 130 miles.

In 1968, when the Badger-G appeared, it carried a missile that looked like a modernized version of the Kennel. It weighed almost 4 tons and had a range of 100 miles. Called the Kelt by NATO, the missile was carried by the Badger-G beneath its wings.

During its long career, the Tu-16 was used in combat many times. Before the outbreak of the Six-Day Arab-Israeli War in June 1967, the Egyptians had received some 25 Tu-16s from the Soviet Union. The Israelis destroyed these planes in the early hours of the conflict. None ever got into the air. After the war, the Soviets replaced the Egyptian losses with new planes that were armed with supersonic Kelt missiles.

In a surprise move on October 6, 1973, Egypt and Syria attacked Israel. The Egyptians crossed the Suez Canal into the Sinai Peninsula, which was then occupied by the Israelis.

During the conflict, Egypt's Tu-16s took to the air and launched their Kelt missiles, each armed with a 2,200-pound warhead. Israeli fighter planes and antiaircraft defenses brought down most of the missiles, but the Kelts destroyed two radar stations and blew up a supply dump. One Tu-16 was shot down.

The war ended on October 24 when a cease-fire was negotiated. Later Israel withdrew from the Canal's west bank. Israel returned the Sinai to Egypt in 1982.

Egypt and the Soviet Union broke off diplomatic relations in 1976. That meant that Egypt could no longer get parts it needed for equipment that had been supplied by the Soviets. But in the case of the Tu-16, Egypt has been able to buy parts from China, which produces its own version of the Tu-16.

More recently, Tu-16s were used by the Soviet Union during its long and bitter war in Afghanistan, which began with the Soviet invasion of that country in 1979. The war did not end until the Soviet Union withdrew the last of its forces in 1989, following a United Nations-negotiated cease-fire agreement the year before.

During the war, the Soviets bombed from high altitudes, beyond the reach of nationalist guerrilla antiaircraft weapons. Tu-16 bombing targets included towns and villages used by the nationalists for rest. Major highways where the nationalists often gathered before attacking were also targeted.

The sizable numbers of Tu-16s now in service, and the fact that the aircraft is still being produced in China, are likely to mean that Tu-16 Badger, in one version or another, is likely to be a factor in military aviation for years to come.

4   GRUMMAN A-6 INTRUDER

Bombing tactics today are much different than they use to be. During World War II, it was standard practice for most bombers, such as the four-engine Boeing B-17 Flying Fortress and Consolidated B-24 Liberator, to gain as much altitude as possible when making a bombing run. The idea, of course, was to get above the antiaircraft fire, or flak. While the technique cut bombing accuracy, Air Force strategists believed they had no choice.

Through the 1950s, bombers continued to use the same tactic, always seeking to fly as high as possible to escape destruction from ground fire, which by then included surface-to-air missiles, or SAMs. Even as late as

A-6 Intruders have been a Navy standby for 30 years. The boomerang-shaped structure jutting from atop the plane's nose is a refueling probe. (U.S. Navy)

A-6 INTRUDER FACT SHEET

Manufacturer: Grumman Aerospace Corporation

Type: Carrier-based long-range attack bomber

Engines: Two Pratt and Whitney J52-P-8B turbojets, each delivering 9,300 pounds of thrust

Crew: Pilot and bombardier/navigator

Length: 54 ft., 7 in.

Height: 16 ft., 2 in.

Wingspan: 53 ft.

Loaded Weight: 60,400 lb.

Performance:

  Maximum Speed: 648 mph

  Service Ceiling: 44,660 ft.

 Range: 1,080 miles

First Flight: 1960

1974, when the prototype for the B-1 bomber took to the air, the policy was still being followed. The B-1 was designed to penetrate enemy airspace at an altitude of 50,000 feet. This was the case in spite of the fact that some SAM systems of the day were effective at an altitude up to 130,000 feet.

The British were the first to understand the foolishness of this policy and do something about it. They realized that the radar signals used in detecting and locating bombers travel in straight lines, so the surest way for an airplane to be spotted by radar was to fly at high altitude. The best way to avoid being seen was to roar in at full speed while keeping very low, at tree-top level, if possible. In so doing, a plane could surprise the enemy by flying under its radar.

In 1952, the British began development of a very fast, low-level, carrier-based bomber that was intended to take advantage of this theory. The result was the twin-engine two-seat Buccaneer, which began service with the Royal Navy's Fleet Air Arm in 1961. The Royal Air Force did not order the aircraft until 1968.

While there were metal fatigue problems with the Buccaneer, it proved highly effective as a multirole strike aircraft. In fact, a number of

Buccaneers are being refitted to extend their usefulness through the 1990s.

In 1956, the U.S. Navy followed the lead of the British, issuing a call for a carrier-based plane to serve as a low-level long-range bomber, one that would be capable of finding and hitting targets in any weather. Of the 11 different designs that were prepared, the Grumman Company's proposal was chosen. It called for a two-engine, midwing, snub-nosed airplane, manned by a crew of two.

The A-6, as it came to be designated, was to be capable of carrying 18,000 pounds of bombs and missiles from five connection points between the wing and fuselage. The aircraft was also to have the capability of delivering nuclear weapons.

The A-6 Intruder first joined the fleet in 1963. Since that time the aircraft's basic airframe has hardly changed. But by looking under the plane's aluminum skin, one gets a very different picture. The aircraft has shown the ability to change with the times, to accommodate the new and ever more sophisticated electronics. It's this ability to be flexible that has enabled the A-6 Intruder to be a key player with the Navy's sea-going forces for some 30 years.

The success of the Intruder—and the British Buccaneer—could not help but influence the design of the big bombers that followed. Even the B-1 was redesigned, although it meant strengthening the plane's airframe and reducing its top speed. The B-1 is now capable of penetrating enemy airspace at the lowest possible level.

A-6s performed heroically during the war in Vietnam. Flying day and night in any weather, they provided United States and South Vietnamese ground forces with close-air support, and attacked enemy troop concentrations, supply columns and fuel storage sites.

The A-6 saw combat for the first time in July 1965 when planes from the carrier *Independence* blasted targets in North Vietnam. Throughout the war, Intruders continued to hit the enemy from the decks of Navy carriers. Manned by Marine Corps pilots, A-6s also flew from bases at Da Nang and Chu Lai.

A single A-6 from the carrier *Constellation* destroyed the Hai Duong Bridge, a major link between Haiphong and Hanoi. Catching the North Vietnamese off guard in what was normally a heavily defended area, the plane cruised in boldly to destroy the bridge's center span with 2,000-pound bombs.

On the night of October 30, 1967, Commander Charles B. Hunter, at the controls of an A-6A, performed one of the most skillful single-

An A-6E lands on the flight deck of the aircraft carrier Coral Sea. (U.S. Navy)

plane strikes of the war. His mission was to attack the Hanoi cargo piers with 500-pound bombs.

Making a low-level, instrument approach, Hunter picked his way through yawning limestone ravines on his way to the target area. Once clear of the limestone formations, Hunter began receiving enemy radar signals. Shortly after, a SAM streaked toward him. With the missile overhead, Hunter dove for his target. But instead of dropping his bombs, he pulled the A-6 into a high "G" barrel roll, a very dangerous maneuver at such a low altitude. The SAM exploded about 200-feet from the aircraft, shaking it up but leaving it undamaged.

As Hunter began his bombing run a second time, more SAMs were fired at him. To avoid them, Hunter went down to almost dock level. The SAMs exploded above him, each causing the plane to shudder and filling the cockpit with orange light.

Hunter bored in, released his bombs, then made a right turn. As he looked back over his shoulder, he could see the bombs falling on the piers.

Besides the A-6 attack plane, two other versions of the Intruder saw action in Vietnam. One was the KA-6A tanker. Fitted with hose-and-reel equipment to provide in-flight refueling, four tankers went to sea with the attack aircraft.

A completely different version of the A-6 was developed in the late 1960s to serve as an electronic countermeasures aircraft. Electronic countermeasures, or ECM, involves the many different techniques used to disrupt or deceive enemy radar and other electronic devices. Jamming, the best known form of ECM, consists of broadcasting loud noises on the same frequency the enemy is using for communications. The result is somewhat the same as when you plug an electric drill or any other heavy appliance into the same electric outlet as your radio. Whatever station you happen to be listening to gets obliterated.

ECM also includes chaff jamming. This is usually accomplished with long strips of aluminum foil that are dropped from an ECM aircraft. The chaff creates an electronic cloud that enemy signals can't penetrate.

ECM equipment can also include computers that are used in collecting information. They study the messages that are being transmitted by the enemy and warn the pilot of any that seem potentially dangerous.

The first of the ECM planes, the EA-6A Prowler, offered over 30 different systems to detect, locate, classify and jam enemy radar transmissions. The two-seat EA-6A, of which 27 were built, was used by the U.S. Marine Corps.

In 1966, the Navy began development of an improved version of the EA-6A. Its fuselage was 4 feet longer and it carried a crew of four, a pilot and three specialists who operated the ECM equipment. The plane was designated the EA-6B.

The chief mission of the new aircraft, which flew for the first time in 1968, was to support the Navy's strike aircraft. Three squadrons of EA-6Bs saw action during the Vietnam War. Following the war, Prowlers were assigned to each of the 12 aircraft carriers then in service and also to Marine air wings.

Through the years, the A-6 Intruder has gone through a good number of model changes. Grumman produced 482 A-6As, all of which have been retired. The A-6B and A-6C, both modified versions of the A-6A, are no longer on active duty, either.

What the Navy flies today is the A-6E, which took to the air for the first time as a prototype in 1970. The first A-6E squadron to be assigned to an aircraft carrier arrived aboard the *Forrestal* in September 1972.

The A-6E features a sophisticated sensor package that enables the Intruder to detect, identify and attack a wide variety of targets, using either conventionally guided or laser-guided weapons. Carried in the plane's small chin turret, this electronics package is known as TRAM, for target recognition and attack multisensor.

The Navy ordered 138 A-6Es. After these were delivered, production continued at the rate of about six planes a year through much of the 1980s.

During the 1980s and into the 1990s, the Navy operated 12 to 14 carrier-based squadrons of A-6Es, with 10 aircraft to a squadron. The U.S. Marine Corps also continued to fly the A-6. The Marines have five squadrons.

In addition to the A-6 squadrons aboard aircraft carriers, the Navy has other Intruder units that do not operate at sea. These aircraft are used chiefly as trainers. They're based at naval air facilities at Oceana, Virginia and Whidbey Island, Washington.

Following air operations aboard the carrier America, *an A-6 Intruder, its wings folded for storage, is lowered to the carrier's hangar deck.*
(George Sullivan)

The U.S. Marine Corps's five squadrons of A-6Es are based at El Toro, California and Cherry Point, North Carolina. Marine Corps A-6 pilots are trained at Cherry Point.

On August 7, 1990, just a few days after Iraq had shocked the world by invading Kuwait, the U.S. Navy aircraft carrier *Independence*, operating in the Gulf of Oman, represented the only American air power available for action.

Meanwhile, the carrier *Eisenhower* was in the eastern Mediterranean Sea and about to enter the Suez Canal on its way to the Persian Gulf. And the carrier *Saratoga* was leaving its homeport of Mayport, Florida, bound for the Mediterranean.

By mid-January 1991, after a massive buildup of troops, supplies and equipment that had gone on for almost five months, the United States had six aircraft carriers stationed in the Persian Gulf and Red Sea. On January 16, 1991, President George Bush announced that "the liberation of Kuwait" had begun and that Desert Storm, the offensive action against Iraq, had been launched.

Four A-6 Intruders from the carrier *Ranger* were in the air within a few hours after the war began. Their target was the Iraqi naval base at Umm Qasr. The lead plane was piloted by Lieutenant Commander Robert Thomson. Lieutenant Commander Rick Price served as bombardier/navigator. Their A-6 carried four high-speed anti-radiation missiles (HARMs) to fire against surface-to-air missile sites.

It was shortly after 5 A.M. when their plane approached Bubiyan Island from the Persian Gulf. A light fog clung to the coastline.

"Thirty seconds to go," said Price. "Steering is on target, system is on attack."

"Roger," replied Thomson. "Coming to steering." He pulled the plane in line with the target, then squeezed the trigger on his stick. THWOOSH! With a blinding flash, the missile shot away from the plane, trailing a glowing plume of smoke as it streaked for its target.

On the first day of Desert Storm, the Navy flew 228 combat sorties. Two planes were lost that day, an A-6 and an F/A-18 fighter attack plane. By the end of the first week of the war, almost all of the Iraq SAM sites had been completely suppressed by HARM missiles or jamming.

To enable them to fly lower and maneuver with greater agility, A-6 pilots operating at night from carriers in the Persian Gulf were equipped with night-vision goggles. With the goggles, A-6 pilots could fly at an altitude of only 200 feet, instead of 600 to 800 feet, which was usual for nighttime operations. Flying at a lower level gave the A-6s an even better chance of avoiding radar detection.

The goggles were about the same as those worn by Army helicopter pilots. They permitted the wearer to see for a distance of 7 miles at night. Because the standard red lighting in the cockpit of the A-6 cut the vision of the goggles, it was replaced with blue-green lighting.

"With goggles, A-6 crews can stay lower longer," said an A-6 training officer. "And they are no longer blind in a sharp turn."

In the target area, however, night goggles did not work very well. "I've found the goggles are good to get you there, and lined up," said one pilot. "But they are a lousy targeting system." To achieve accuracy, A-6 crews switched back to radar, infrared and laser bombing systems when close to their targets.

A-6s in the Persian Gulf also made use of tactical air launched decoys, or TALDs. These were 10-foot gliders that were carried and launched just as if they were 500-pound bombs. Each decoy could be programmed to simulate the radar signature of an aircraft or an air-launched weapon. Not only did the enemy fire expensive antiaircraft missiles at the decoys, they used their radar to try to detect them, which made their radar systems easy targets for antiradiation missiles.

Some A-6s are land based. Here an Intruder taxis to the flight line at the Cubi Point Naval Air Station in the Philippines. (U.S. Navy)

Some of the A-6s carried two of the decoys in addition to their bombloads. But other Intruders were loaded with as many as 20 of the TALDs in an effort to overload enemy radar systems.

The bombing of Iraq continued for about six weeks. A-6s were in the air virtually every day and night. They attacked and destroyed artillery batteries, aircraft that the Iraqis had attempted to hide behind embankments, tankers, patrol boats, mine-laying boats, launching craft and even a hovercraft.

During the late 1980s, Navy officials made plans to replace the A-6 with the A-12 attack aircraft, which was to be a stealth plane. Stealth technology is a combination of design and materials that absorb or deflect radar signals so as to reduce the radar cross section of a plane. In a sense, the plane becomes invisible to radar. The Air Force has a stealth fighter in the F-117, which won high praise for its achievements during the Persian Gulf war. It also has the B-2 Stealth bomber, which flew for the first time in 1989. But in January 1991, Secretary of Defense Richard Cheney canceled the A-12 because of delays and high costs.

Cheney's decision left the Navy with no stealth aircraft and no replacement for the A-6. Another attack aircraft, the AX, also a stealth plane, loomed as another choice for the Navy. But the AX will not be available until the end of the 1990s.

Earlier, Grumman had sought to extend the life of the Intruder with the development of the A-6F. This model had a narrower nose, new engines and improved radar. The A-6F was first flown in 1987. However, the project was canceled before the end of the decade.

But there is an innovation that has added years of life to the A-6. Boeing Military Airplanes, a division of the Boeing Company, developed an unusual wing for the A-6. Made of a mix of graphite and epoxy, it is stronger than the plane's original aluminum wing and offers greater resistance to corrosion.

Titanium is used in areas of high stress for added strength. The entire structure is covered with a nickle-based fabric to ward off lightning strikes.

The first flight of an A-6E with the new wing took place on April 3, 1989. The job of replacing old wings with new ones began in the 1990s. The new wing is expected to add 8,000 flight hours, or about 15 years, to the operation of the A-6E. As this suggests, the Intruder seems certain to remain in service with the Navy and the Marine Corps well into the next century.

5 DASSAULT-BREGUET MIRAGE IV

A two-seat, supersonic, delta-wing tactical strike aircraft, France's Mirage IV was designed to do just one job: deliver a nuclear weapon. When the plane entered service in 1964, that weapon was a free-fall nuclear bomb. In 1986, the Mirage IV was completely remodeled to enable it to carry, not a bomb, but an impressive long-range missile. The missile has its own navigation system that permits it to make sharp turns and evasive maneuvers. But, like the bomb, it has a nuclear warhead.

The Mirage IV is a close cousin to the Mirage III, the French fighter plane with a glowing international reputation. Designed more than 30 years ago, the Mirage III, in various updated versions, not only continues to serve the Armee de l'Air (the French Air Force), but is also the mainstay of some two dozen other air forces of the world. First built as an interceptor for the Armee de l'Air, the plane has been successfully

With its delta wing and slim fuselage, the Mirage IV is one of the "cleanest" bombers ever built. (National Air & Space Museum)

45

MIRAGE IV FACT SHEET

Manufacturer: Dassault-Breguet, France

Type: Strategic bomber and missile carrier

Engines: Two SNECMA Atar 09K after-burning turbojets, each delivering 15,432 pounds of thrust

Crew: Pilot and navigator

Length: 77 ft., 1 in.

Height: 17 ft., 9 in.

Wingspan: 38 ft., 10½ in.

Loaded Weight: 73,800 lb.

Performance:

   Maximum Speed: 1,454 mph

   Service Ceiling: 60,000 ft.

   Range: 770 miles

First Flight: 1963

---

converted into a tactical strike aircraft as well as a photo reconnaissance plane.

Like the Mirage III, the Mirage IV has a delta wing and slim fuselage. But the Mirage IV is a considerably larger plane, has two engines (not merely one), a crew of two (not one). It also has a much more sophisticated radar and navigation system.

During the mid-1960s, the Armee de l'Air ordered 62 Mirage IVs, which were assigned to three *escadres* (wings): the French Air Force's 91st Squadron at Mont-de-Marsan, the 93rd Squadron at Istres and a third unit at St. Dizier, east of Paris.

Like most of the other bombers developed during the late 1950s, the Mirage IV was designed to fly very fast and very high. But as radar became more sophisticated and began detecting and tracking high-flying aircraft or surface-to-air missiles, planes were forced to come down in order to survive.

Flying at low levels creates problems, however. It subjects the airframe to violent buffeting. The rough ride quickly tires the pilot and other crew members. They have difficulty doing their jobs with their usual efficiency.

To go toward a target at a low level requires a plane with a strong airframe and short wings. It also demands special radar that can navigate the aircraft over the contours of the land, avoiding all obstructions.

Besides the Mirage, there are only a couple of aircraft that have these qualities. One is the U.S. Air Force's F-111, a plane with variable swept wings and tremendous speed and range. The F-111 won loud praise for its performance in Vietnam and, more recently, in the Persian Gulf. Panavia's Tornado (see p. 80) is another strike aircraft that can attack at low level. It is flown by Great Britain's Royal Air Force as well as the Royal Saudi Air Force.

Another problem when attacking at low levels, where the air is much more dense, is the rate of fuel consumption increases, which means the plane's range can be sharply reduced. Mirage IV crew members solved this problem by means of a unique "buddy" system of in-flight refueling. A slender in-flight refueling probe was mounted in the nose of each Mirage IV. Mirage missions were planned using planes in pairs. One plane carried the mission's bombs or missiles; the other carried an over-supply of fuel, plus hose-and-drum refilling equipment.

Fuel, of course, could also be supplied by tanker planes operated by the Armee de l'Air. But such aircraft are not likely to go along on a combat mission because they present too big of a target.

During the 1970s, France began developing a long-range nuclear missile that had a range of at least 62 miles and a self-contained navigation system. To deliver the missile, 18 of the original 62 Mirage IVs were completely rebuilt and given advanced radar and navigation systems and electronics-jamming and chaff-dispensing systems.

These planes entered service with the Armee de l'Air in 1986. They are expected to remain on active duty until the turn of the century.

Because it often flies at ground-hugging levels, where the air is more dense, the Mirage IV requires frequent refueling. (National Air & Space Museum)

Most of the remaining Mirage IVs have been withdrawn from active duty. An additional 12, however, have been rebuilt as reconnaissance aircraft. They have been fitted out with radar, sensors and, of course, cameras. Some of the bigger sensors are carried in a large externally mounted pod.

Besides the United States and the independent states of the former Soviet Union, France is the only other nation to be able to deliver nuclear weapons in three different ways—by launching them from underground silos, by launching them from submarines and by releasing them from strategic bombers.

The Mirage IV is what gives France its air delivery capability. The nation is likely to maintain this capability in its present form for some time to come.

6   FAIRCHILD-REPUBLIC A-10 THUNDERBOLT

Everyone agrees what makes a good weapon: It has to be effective, that is, able to do its job better than whatever the enemy puts up against it. It has to be reliable and easy to operate. It also has to be reasonably priced so it can be purchased in large quantities.

All of these qualities are combined in the low-flying, slow-flying A-10 Thunderbolt II, a single-seat attack aircraft known affectionately as the

Besides the 30-mm cannon jutting out from beneath its nose, this A-10 carries four AGM-65 Maverick missiles. (U.S. Air Force)

A-10 THUNDERBOLT II FACT SHEET

Prime Contractor: Fairchild Republic Company

Type: Short-range close-support attack aircraft

Engines: Two General Electric TF34-GE-100 turbofans, each
delivering 9,065 pounds of thrust

Crew: Pilot

Length: 53 ft., 4 in.

Height: 14 ft., 8 in.

Wingspan: 57 ft., 6 in.

Loaded Weight: 50,000 lb.

Performance:

    Maximum Speed: 439 mph

    Service Ceiling: (NA)

    Range: 288 miles

First Flight: 1974

"Warthog." As a close-support airplane, it is the U.S. Air Force's chief antitank weapon.

Late in the 1960s, when the Air Force began developing the aircraft that was to become the A-10, it started at square one. The experts asked themselves, What's a close-support aircraft supposed to do? Its job is to swoop low over the battlefield and mow down enemy tanks and other vehicles.

At the time, the Air Force had a gun whose shells could penetrate tank armor, a gun that was a terrific tank buster. It was a huge 30-mm Gatling gun, with seven revolving barrels packed in a tight cluster. Each barrel loaded and fired automatically as the cylinder-shaped package turned.

The gun fired shells the size of Coke bottles. The shells were special. They were made of used-up, or spent, uranium. They were not radio-active, but they were very, very heavy. That's what enabled them to slice through thick armor plate. At practice ranges, the shells regularly uprooted the timbers that supported the targets.

The gun could spew out 70 shells a second. It could kill a tank with a 35-shell burst.

Another advantage of the gun, which was designated the GAU-8A Avenger, was economy. Its shells cost far less than bombs or missiles. In addition, an airplane could carry more of them.

Air Force designers realized that this Gatling gun was what they needed. So the designers built the plane around the gun.

The designers first looked back to the Vietnam and Mideast wars and examined the reasons why close-support aircraft were lost during those wars. They found that most of the losses—some 62 percent—were caused by fuel fires and explosions.

In planning the A-10, they made sure that the four fuel tanks would be separated and they surround them with fire resistant foam. They filled the tanks with a spongy foam. Should a fuel tank be split open by enemy fire, the fuel wouldn't gush out of it.

In most aircraft, fuel is stored in the wings, which are easy targets in a ground-support plane. The wing tanks of the A-10 are tucked in close to the fuselage, and it is the fuel in these tanks that the aircraft uses first. By the time the plane has taxied, taken off and flown to the target area, the wing tanks are dry.

The A-10's two main fuel tanks are protected by armor plating. The plane's fuel lines are self-sealing. Fire walls prevent engine fire from spreading to the fuel tanks.

The designers of the new plane found the second biggest reason for losses was damage to aircraft engines and flight controls from antiaircraft fire. For that reason, they decided to move the A-10's two engines to a position above the fuselage, so as to be at least partially protected by it. Aviation writer Michael Skinner says the engines "look as though they've been stuck on the A-10 as an afterthought."

The engines are widely separated, too. Enemy fire that hits one isn't likely to knock out the other.

Eighteen percent of the losses the designers examined occurred because the pilot got hit and could no longer fly the aircraft. So in the A-10 the pilot is given plenty of protection. He sits within a bathtub-shaped pocket that encloses the entire cockpit. It is made of titanium, one of the hardest metals known.

Designers fired round after round of high-explosive 23-mm shells at the armored bathtub. The outer surface merely discolored.

Then they fired 37-mm high-incendiary rounds at the bathtub. These made slight dents but failed to pierce the armor.

Designers made the pilot's controls "triple redundant." That means there are three sets of controls. If two should happen to get shot away, the pilot can still fly the plane with the third.

A-10 Thunderbolts from Osan Air Base fly in formation during joint maneuvers in Korea carried out by the United States and the Republic of Korea. (U.S. Air Force)

The plans called for the plane to be a slow mover, one that could carry its big gun and a heavy load of ammunition and weapons a distance of some 230 miles, remain in the battle zone for an hour or two attacking enemy targets time and again, then return to its base.

The designers realized that such a plane was going to take more than its share of hits from enemy ground fire. Over the battlefield, the idea is to move fast, not slow. So instead of giving the aircraft speed, they compensated by making it exceptionally easy to handle. The plane was designed to be able to fly very close to the ground so it could duck around buildings, clusters of trees, or any other cover. And once it had launched an attack, it would be able to turn away quickly, making its escape before the enemy even realized what had happened.

Even with these qualities, it was realized that the plane was not going to be able to escape enemy fire on every mission. It was therefore built to be a survivor, to take a hit or two and keep flying. In fact, it was built to be able to return to its base with half a wing, and a tail section and one engine missing.

As part of the Air Force's development program for the aircraft, both the Fairchild Company and the Northrop Corporation built prototypes. The Fairchild prototype flew for the first time on May 10, 1977, and the following year Fairchild was named the winner of the design competition. Eventually the Air Force ordered 707 production models of the plane, which was designated the A-10 Thunderbolt II.

To help them survive during operations over the modern-day battlefield, many A-10 pilots were given Joint Attack Weapons Systems (JAWS) training at Fort Benning, Georgia or Fort Ord, California. In these exercises, A-10 pilots were drilled in working with Army helicopters.

Helicopters can do some things the A-10 can't do. They can hover out of sight, then suddenly pop up to take a look around and fire a few rounds. But helicopters are easy to bring down and are limited in the type of weapons they can carry. For example, helicopters can't handle the Maverick missiles that the A-10 carries, nor can a helicopter be expected to tote the A-10's 30-mm gun, which weighs 2 tons.

In the JAWS exercises, artillery fire was called upon first. This helped to confuse the enemy tanks and kept them "buttoned up," unable to use their heavy machine guns.

Then the helicopters went in, keeping very low, almost scraping the earth, exposing themselves to fire only when attacking.

The A-10s followed close behind the helicopters, also staying low. They opened fire at a range of 2,500 feet, and stopped firing at 1,200 feet. The A-10 would have been more accurate if it fired from closer ranges, of course. But the A-10 pilots couldn't get too close to their targets. Otherwise, they ran the risk of being hit with jagged hunks of exploding metal that result when those 30-mm shells smacked into a tank or other armored target.

The first combat-ready A-10 squadron—the 356th Tactical Fighter Squadron—was established at Myrtle Beach Air Force Base, South Carolina in 1977. In the years that followed, the A-10 often received overseas assignments. Thunderbolt IIs were stationed at Royal Air Force bases in England and at American air bases in West Germany. Eighteen A-10s were also assigned to South Korea, arriving at Suwon Air Base in 1982.

During the war in the Persian Gulf, the A-10 was given a different mission by the Air Force. Instead of waiting until the ground war began and then using the Warthog to protect U.S. troops in battle, the Air Force pushed the plane into action right at the beginning. A-10s were used to fly patrols over Iraq and Kuwait, searching for ground targets— tanks, Scud missile-launching sites or moving convoys.

In addition to the 30-mm cannon, A-10s in the Persian Gulf were armed with the AGM-65 Maverick missile, which is controlled by the pilot. He selects the target on his TV cockpit display and the missile flies toward it. A-10s in the Persian Gulf also carried 500-pound Mark 82 gravity bombs and cluster bombs. These split open in midair to send down more than 200 "bomblets" in an area the size of a football field.

On the first day of the war, the A-10s hit their targets with ease. "This is going to be pretty much a turkey shoot," said one pilot.

But then thick clouds rolled in over the desert. They blotted out the Iraqi Army and armor for more than six days. When the clouds finally lifted, the A-10 pilots discovered that the situation had changed. The Iraqi military had dug in. "He's buried his whole army," said one pilot, referring to Saddam Hussein, president of Iraq.

"What you were looking for in Vietnam was hiding under the trees," another pilot said. "Here it's hiding under the sand."

Sometimes a lightly armed observer aircraft would be sent out in advance of the A-10s. Designated OA-10s, these planes fired a white phosphorous rocket when one of them spotted a tank, convoy or other target. Then an A-10 would be sent in to destroy it.

The 335th Tactical Fighter Squadron, an A-10 unit from Myrtle Beach, South Carolina, flew almost exclusively at night. Flying in the darkness without lights, the members of the squadron had to take special precautions to keep out of each other's way. There was even a chance they could "mort themselves out," pilot slang for shooting one another accidentally.

The A-10's engines are mounted above the fuselage so as to be protected by it from antiaircraft fire from the ground. (U.S. Air Force)

The pilots stacked themselves at different altitudes. They also kept in constant touch over their radios, using well-known reference points to keep themselves away from one another.

One night, relying chiefly on their nose-mounted cannons, the A-10s attacked an Iraqi armored convoy, destroying 24 tanks. "It was a busy night," one pilot said jokingly.

One plane limped back to its base after an Iraqi missile or artillery fire had torn a gaping hole in its wing. "Everything was sucked out the wing," said a mechanic who inspected the plane. "Any other aircraft would not have made it back."

Like any pilot at the controls of an aircraft that flies low and slow, A-10 pilots worried most about the "Golden BB." That was the slang term used for any unlikely shot that strikes a pilot or his plane. It could be, for instance, the single shot fired by a soldier in a foxhole who saw an airplane, pointed his assault weapon at it and pulled the trigger.

Pilots in strike planes, blazing along at supersonic speeds at 40,000 feet, don't have to be concerned about the Golden BB. "Speed is life" is their motto.

When there are dozens of soldiers on the battlefield below or, worse, hundreds of them, the A-10 pilot becomes even more fearful of the Golden BB. He takes consolation in the fact that he's sitting in that titanium bathtub.

"Golden BB" wasn't the only slang term to come out of the Persian Gulf war. Air crew members, returning from a mission, would discuss what they called the "triple A," or "A.A.A.," meaning antiaircraft artillery, the fire from machine guns and cannons.

Missiles were often described by acronyms, by words formed from the first letters of other words. SAM, an acronym that dates to the Vietnam War, was a surface-to-air missile. TOW referred to a tube-launched, optically traced, wire-guided (missile). SLAM stood for standoff land attack missile.

Scud, the missile the Iraqis launched toward Israel and other targets, was not an acronym. Scud was a NATO code word for the Russian built missile.

The term "carpet bombing" was often used in connection with B-52 missions. It referred to what occurred when bombs were dropped over a large area rather than toward a specific target.

"Fur ball" was the term used to describe a dogfight, an aerial battle between fighter planes.

During a fur ball, a pilot battled a "bogie," an enemy aircraft. "I don't know if the bogie was chasing him," an American pilot said after a mission, "but I locked him up, confirmed he was hostile, and fired a missile."

To "lock him up" or "lock on" means to fix a weapon on a target by means of an electronic system.

Within three weeks after the air attack began, the landscape of Iraq and Kuwait was pocked with bomb craters and littered with destroyed armored vehicles. One A-10 pilot noted that during the first week of the war he used up his supply of cluster bombs, Maverick missiles and 500-pound bombs in just one pass over the battlefield. After three or four weeks, it required six or seven passes to find enough targets to use up his arsenal.

As the bombing increased, American airmen began to complain that they were having difficulty finding target areas that had not already been bombed. "We're starting to see miles of blackened earth and bomb craters," said one pilot. "And little else."

That's when military planners decided to change tactics. They issued new maps of Kuwait and southern Iraq that were divided into boxes, with each box representing an area about 20 miles long and wide. "Killing boxes," is what pilots called them. Each was identified with a series of letters and numbers.

The idea was to make the bombing more methodical. As Iraqi tanks, artillery positions, and storage facilities were destroyed in one box, allied aircraft moved on to the next.

The A-10's fuselage is sometimes given this adornment. (U.S. Air Force)

Then another problem developed. Allied warplanes were spending too much time picking out the cleverly hidden and often partially buried targets within the boxes.

Lieutenant General Charles A. Horner, who commanded allied air forces, had a solution to that problem. He ordered veteran A-10 fighter pilots to scout the areas to be bombed in advance. These "Killer Scouts," as they came to be called, spent the daylight hours patrolling the boxes, seeking out tanks, artillery and troop concentrations. Then they would report what they found to allied attack planes. This strategy enabled the A-10s, F-16s and other aircraft to fly more missions.

To some observers of the Persian Gulf war, the unlovely Warthog did not seem to belong in the same Air Force that featured such aircraft as the swift and sinister looking B-2 Stealth and the speedy and nimble F-16 Flying Falcon. (Before the Persian Gulf war, the Air Force had agreed to turn most of its A-10s over to the Army.) "I think it's the ugliest airplane we've built," one Air Force officer said. "But it's also the meanest looking . . . especially when you're looking down that gun barrel."

7   TUPOLEV Tu-22 BLINDER

Unveiled in 1961, the Tu-22 Blinder was the Soviet Union's first supersonic bomber. (National Air & Space Museum)

On Aviation Day in Moscow in 1961, the Soviet Union introduced several previously unknown aircraft, the existence of which jolted the United States and its allies. The greatest shock of all was provided by a big and powerful supersonic bomber, the Tu-22, the first aircraft of its kind in the Soviet arsenal. No fewer than 10 examples of the giant aircraft were put on display that day.

Tu-22 FACT SHEET

Designer: Tupolev OKB

Type: Twin-engine medium-range supersonic bomber

Engines: Two Koliesov VD-7 turbojets, each delivering 39,900 lb. of thrust

Crew: Pilot, systems engineer and navigator

Length: 132 ft., 11½ in.

Height: 35 ft.

Wingspan: 78 ft.

Loaded Weight: 185,000 lb.

Performance:

  Maximum Speed: 920 mph

  Service Ceiling: 60,000 ft.

  Range: 1,800 miles

First Flight: 1959

Nine of the planes were conventional bombers but one had been modified to carry a supersonic missile under its belly. Called the Kitchen missile by NATO, it cruised at better than twice the speed of sound and had a range of 400 miles. It was also known to have a very accurate radar homing system.

Classified as a medium bomber, the new aircraft were given the name Beauty by NATO. But since NATO didn't want any of its names to sound complimentary, it was later changed to Blinder.

No matter what name happened to be used, the aircraft and its close cousin, the Tu-22M Backfire (see p. 61), were a cause of great concern to the American military for close to three decades, or until the breakup of the Soviet Union in 1991. Whenever trouble flared in the Middle East or in Africa, the Tu-22 Blinder, flown by pilots representing nations allied with the Soviet Union, usually played a role.

The history of the Tu-22 Blinder goes back the 1950s. On November 11, 1956, the U.S. Air Force introduced the B-58 Hustler, the world's first bomber capable of blazing through the sky faster than the speed of sound. A sleek, delta-winged aircraft, the B-58 was even speedier than most fighters of the time.

Even before the B-58 was flown for the first time, the Soviet Union knew of the plane and sought to meet the challenge it presented. By 1956, a prototype had been developed by the Soviets and called the Tu-98. This design was replaced by a bigger, more powerful version of the aircraft, which became the Tu-22.

The different versions of the Tu-22 were to include:

Blinder-A—The original bomber, first seen in 1961. The aircraft was capable of carrying 22,000 pounds of bombs or missiles, either conventional or nuclear, in its fuselage weapons bay.

Blinder-B—While similar to the Blinder-A, this plane had a weapons bay that was modified to carry the Kitchen cruise missile, which could be fitted with either a nuclear or conventional warhead. The Blinder-B also had increased radar capability.

Blinder-C—This was the naval reconnaissance version of the plane. It was fitted with six camera windows in the weapons bay doors, plus special equipment to enable the aircraft to play a role in gathering electronic intelligence. Electronic countermeasures may have been one of its duties. Blinder Cs, operating from shore bases, served the Soviet Navy, chiefly in the Baltic Sea and the Black Sea.

Blinder-D—This was the training version of the Tu-22, equipped with an added cockpit for the instructor, located just behind the flight deck.

The Soviet Union supplied Iraq with a dozen Tu-22s in 1974. They were used on bombing missions by the Iraqis during that nation's fierce war with Iran, which lasted from 1980 to 1988. The planes were also believed to have been used against villages occupied by the Kurdish minority in Iraq.

The Soviets also delivered Tu-22 Blinder-B bombers to Libya. They may have been used in that nation's effort to occupy and control Chad, Libya's neighbor just to the south. One Tu-22 is said to have carried out an attack on an airfield in Chad after first simulating the approach of a commercial airliner.

The U.S. Air Force never had great success with the B-58 Hustler. The plane proved very costly to operate and by 1971 had been retired. But about 75 Tu-22s remained in active service. As for the Tu-22's successor, the Tu-22M Backfire, more than 350 served with the Soviet Air Force, and production continued at the rate of about 30 planes a year until 1991.

8   TUPOLEV Tu-22M BACKFIRE

While scanning vast stretches of the Soviet Union in 1969, an American satellite photographed the prototype of a big new bomber parked outside a huge factory at Kazan in western Russia. While the aircraft resembled the Tu-22 Blinder, it featured variable-geometry wings. No Blinder ever had "swing wings," as they are sometimes called.

While it has similarities to the Tu-22 Blinder, the variable-wing Tu-22M Backfire is a vastly different aircraft. (National Air & Space Museum)

Variable wings help a plane perform at its very best. When the plane is cruising or racing through the sky at high altitude, the wings are swept

TU-22M FACT SHEET

Contractor: Tupolev OKB

Type: Twin-engine medium-range supersonic bomber

Engines: Two Kuznetsov NK-144 turbofans, each developing 44,090 lb. of thrust

Crew: Two pilots side by side, systems engineer and navigator/bombardier

Length: 129 ft., 11 in.

Height: 33 ft., 5¼ in.

Wingspan:

    Fully Spread 112 ft. 6½ in.

    Fully Swept: 76 ft., 9¼ in.

Loaded Weight: 286,600 lb.

Performance:

    Maximum Speed: 1,265 mph

    Service Ceiling: 60,000 ft.

    Range: 3,400 miles

First Flown: Fall 1969

---

back, lessening the plane's resistance to the air and thus working to increase its speed. When the plane is landing or taking off, and needs all the lift it can get, the wings are spread wide.

Careful study of the satellite photo showed that the new plane, which later would be designated the Tu-22M Backfire, was a rebuilt version of the Tu-22 Blinder. But compared to the original model of the Tu-22, the Backfire proved to be a great deal more efficient. Thanks to its variable geometry wings, it could take off and land in less than half the distance required by the original model of the Tu-22.

The Soviets kept working to improve the Backfire. Andrei N. Tupolev, the most noted of the Soviet Union's aircraft designers, headed the team working on the plane. Tupolev died in 1972, at just about the time the improved model of the aircraft was reaching completion.

Although there were still similarities to the original Tu-22 Blinder, the new version was essentially a wholly different aircraft. Besides the swing-wing feature, there were much more powerful engines, which provided for great fuel efficiency. The whole aircraft had been strengthened to enable it to carry much more fuel and a bigger weapons payload.

The crew's accommodations were different, too. In the original version of the plane, there was a separate compartment for the navigator/bombardier. This was replaced by a seating arrangement that included two pairs of ejection seats. The front pair was occupied by the pilot and copilot, the rear pair by the navigator/bombardier and the systems engineer.

Because of its ability to deliver nuclear weapons over very long distances, the Backfire became a much discussed subject during SALT (Strategic Arms Limitation Talks) discussions between the Soviet Union and the United States. These negotiations, which began in 1969, were aimed at putting a limit on the production of nuclear weapons.

The first round of meetings was completed in 1972. The second round lasted from 1973 to 1979.

When President Richard Nixon visited Moscow in 1972, the United States and the Soviet Union signed important agreements that had resulted from the SALT. One was a treaty that put a limit on each country's defensive missile system. The other agreement limited the production of certain nuclear weapons.

In 1979, when Jimmy Carter was president, the United States and the Soviets signed another SALT treaty limiting the production of missiles and long-range bombers. This agreement stated that the Soviets could produce no more than 30 Backfires a year. But the treaty never took effect because the U.S. Senate did not ratify it.

Late in 1979, the Soviet Union launched a massive attack on Afghanistan, a neighboring country to the south, in an effort to take over the country. In part to protest the Soviet's invasion, the Senate stopped considering the SALT treaty. The fighting in Afghanistan continued until 1988, when an agreement that had been hammered out by the United Nations was signed. It provided for the Soviet forces to withdraw from Afghanistan. By early 1989, the withdrawal was completed.

During the 1980s, the Tu-22M Backfire continued to be a controversial topic during talks between the Soviet Union and the United States. The United States argued that the Tu-22 was intended chiefly for strategic attacks on North America. The Soviet said that it wasn't, that the plane was intended to be used only on a regional basis. To bolster their argument, the Soviets removed the plane's nose-mounted fuel boom (which was essential for refueling and reaching the North American continent). It could have been reinstalled in a matter of minutes, however.

Despite what the Soviets said, American military leaders continued to look upon the Backfire, the biggest and most powerful Soviet airplane of its day, as an alarming weapon. It was said that the Tu-22 was a strategic bomber and missile carrier aimed at the very heart of America.

While it was true that the Backfire, with in-flight refueling, did have the capability of attacking the United States mainland, that did not seem to be the principal reason for which it was created. All important targets in the United States had long been covered by Soviet land-based missiles. The Soviets had other uses for their manned bombers.

One of them involved naval ships. Because they're always on the move, aircraft carriers, guided missile cruisers, destroyers and all the rest are not reasonable targets for strategic missiles. But they are vulnerable to long-range aircraft, such as the Tu-22M Backfire. Nearly all examples of the Backfire intercepted by NATO fighter planes during the 1980s belonged to Soviet Naval Aviation.

Like all Soviet combat planes, the Backfire was heavily equipped with defensive electronics systems. Much of the plane's outer skin was covered with receivers and jammers.

In 1989, these three versions of the Backfire were identified:

Tu-22M-1—This was the original production model of the aircraft. Not more than 12 were built.

Tu-22M-2—The first of the swing-wing Backfires, it carried three Kitchen cruise missiles, each with a 1-ton conventional or nuclear warhead. Maximum range of the missile was approximately 270 miles.

With modifications to the weapons bay, the Tu-22M-2 could carry some 12 tons of free-fall weapons, including nuclear arms and naval mines. For defense, the aircraft was equipped with a pair of 23-mm twin-barrel guns. One was mounted above the other in the tail.

Tu-22M-3—The advanced production model of the aircraft, this model went into service with the Black Sea Fleet in 1985. Among its advances were wedge-shaped air intakes, similar to those of the MiG-25 Foxbat, a high-altitude interceptor. Wider than the previous intakes, these made for increased airflow and greater range and power. Instead of a fuel probe, the Tu-22M-3 carried a nose pod containing advanced electronics.

Between 350 and 400 Tu-22M-2s and 3s were in service in 1990. About two-thirds of these aircraft were lined up against NATO forces in Europe and over the Atlantic. The others were based in the Soviet Union's far east and were often seen east of the Korean peninsula. They were thus of some concern to the Japanese.

As either a bomber or missile carrier, the Tu-22M Backfire was looked upon as a formidable opponent. Indeed, no aircraft in the Soviet arsenal was the cause of so much anxiety.

By early 1990s, 350 to 400 swing-wing Backfires were in service. (National Air & Space Museum)

9 LTV A-7 CORSAIR II

It was 1964 and the war in Vietnam was beginning to heat up, when a design team from the Chance Vought Corporation (now the LTV Corporation) set to work to develop a carrier-based strike aircraft that was to reflect, at least in part, some of the lessons being learned in the war. The plane had to have a first class navigation system and the ability to carry a heavy weapons load. It had to be able to cope with Soviet-built MiG fighters, surface-to-air missiles and antiaircraft fire. It did not have to be pretty.

Nor did the aircraft have to be able to fly at supersonic speed, even though other warplanes of the day, the F-105 Thunderchief, for one, were capable of hurrying through the sky faster than the speed of sound.

The A-7 Corsair II was a mainstay of the Navy's arsenal for well over 20 years. (George Sullivan)

A-7E CORSAIR FACT SHEET

Manufacturer: LTV Aircraft Products Group

Type: Carrier-based light attack bomber

Engine: One Allison TF41-A-2 turbofan delivering 14,250 pounds of thrust

Crew: Pilot

Length: 46 ft., 1½ in.

Height: 16 ft., 1 in.

Wingspan: 38 ft., 9 in.

Loaded Weight: 42,000 lb.

Performance:

    Maximum Speed: 698 mph

    Service Ceiling: 51,000 ft.

    Range: 700 miles

First Flight: 1965

But the Navy reasoned that a supersonic aircraft needed more fuel to be able to fight at low altitudes. Having less fuel available would put a limit on the time the aircraft could spend at the target.

There was also an economic reason to make the plane subsonic. The Navy said it would be able to purchase three subsonic aircraft for what it cost to buy just one supersonic plane.

Early in 1964, Chance Vought began production of the first prototype. The company based its design on the F-8 Crusader, a carrier-based fighter the company had begun producing in the late 1950s. The A-7, however, was to have a shorter fuselage than the F-8, no afterburner and less sweepback in the wings.

Overall, the new aircraft was strengthened to allow the wings and fuselage to carry a load of weapons totaling 15,000 pounds, which was enormous by standards of the day. It was about three times the bombload of World War II heavy bombers and twice that of the A-4 Skyhawk, the plane the A-7 was to replace.

What the design team produced was a bulky, clumsy-looking plane, sometimes called the SLUF, for "short little ugly fella." The first prototype flew on September 27, 1964. On November 10 that year, the A-7 was officially named the Corsair II, which honored the F-4U Corsair, a World War II Navy fighter with an unusual bent-wing design. More Corsairs were built—12,620 of them—than any other World War II U.S. fighter plane.

During test flights of the A-7 prototypes, no major problems developed, although pilots complained the new plane seemed underpowered at times. One pilot expressed concern over the plane's lack of power, saying the A-7s bombload was "too big for its own good." Another problem was that the plane was hard to handle on wet runways. The A-7 made its first carrier takeoffs and landings aboard the *America* on November 15, 1965.

The A-7 didn't impress anyone at first. No one dreamed the stubby little plane would become a mainstay of the Navy's arsenal for more than two decades or that the plane would see combat on five different occasions—in Vietnam, Lebanon, Grenada, Libya and the Persian Gulf.

Only 28 months after its first flight, the A-7 was ordered into action. On December 4, 1967, A-7s from the carrier *Ranger*, armed with Zuni rockets, attacked North Vietnamese bridges and highways.

In the first two months of operations over Vietnam, A-7 squadrons from the *Ranger* flew 1,400 missions, losing only one aircraft. It was thought to have been brought down by a SAM missile near Haiphong. The pilot, Lieutenant Commander J. M. Hickerson, was captured by the North Vietnamese after he ejected. He remained a captive until 1973, when he returned home with other American POWs.

During late 1967 and early 1968, the A-7 was also flown into combat from the carrier *Ranger* by Air Force pilots. They found the plane to be rugged and "long-legged," meaning it could travel a good distance without refueling. But they considered the engine weak, although it required relatively little fuel. To maintenance mechanics personnel, the A-7 was a cinch to work on.

Another advantage of the A-7 was that it could deliver just about every weapon in the Navy's inventory. These included MK-81 Snakeye bombs, Walleye glide bombs, 2,000-pound bombs, Shrike missiles, Bullpup missiles and the aforementioned Zuni rockets.

During the period the plane served in Vietnam, the A-7 went through several stages of development. The A-7A, the first model of the aircraft, was also the first to see action in Vietnam. The Navy ordered 199 A-7As.

The A-7B, which was very similar to the A-7A, except for an improved engine, first flew in February 1968. The Navy ordered 196 A-7Bs.

The A-7C, of which 67 were ordered, served as a two-seat training model of the plane. The A-7D was built, not for the Navy, but for the

A pair of A-7 Corsair IIs from the carrier Constellation. (LTV Aircraft Products)

Air Force. It was also flown by the Air National Guard units in 10 states, plus Puerto Rico.

The A-7D offered a more powerful engine and improved electronics. Bombing and navigational systems were computerized. More protective armor was another of the plane's innovations. A total of 459 A-7Ds were ordered by the Air Force.

For self-protection, the A-7D was equipped with the M-61 Vulcan 20-mm cannon, which was mounted up front on the left side of the fuselage. The gun could fire 6,000 rounds per minute.

In March 1970, the A-7D demonstrated what "long legs" it had. Two of the planes made the 3,502-mile flight from Edwards Air Force Base, California to Homestead Air Force Base, Florida without refueling. The addition of external fuel tanks were what enabled the aircraft to fly such a long distance.

In September 1970, the 354th Tactical Fighter Wing at Myrtle Beach Air Force Base, South Carolina became the first of the Air Force's operational wings to receive the A-7D.

The 354th Tactical Squadron Fighter Wing shifted operations to Vietnam in 1972. Between October 16 and the end of the year, when

American participation in Vietnam came to a halt, A-7Ds, which were based at the Korat Royal Thai Air Force Base in Thailand, flew some 4,000 missions.

Thanks to its tremendous range, the A-7D was able to operate while fully combat loaded throughout all of South Vietnam and most of North Vietnam. Besides bombing raids, the A-7D flew search-and-rescue missions and also night escort missions for AC-130 gunships.

The A-7E was the Navy's final version of the plane. The model was first flown in November 1968. Eventually 535 A-7Es were ordered. The plane had many of the qualities of the Air Force's A-7D, including its 20-mm gun and the ability to carry 7 to 8 tons of bombs and missile.

A-7s served in combat in Vietnam for 49 months, flying more than 100,000 missions. A total of 55 planes were lost.

During the 1980s, the United States often squared off against Libya and its head of state, Colonel Muammar al-Qaddafi. President Ronald Reagan accused Libya of masterminding many international terrorist attacks.

Early in 1985, Colonel Qaddafi established a "line of death" across the northern border of the Gulf of Sidra, an inlet of the Mediterranean Sea on the northern coast of Libya. He warned the line was not to be crossed.

In March of that year, to demonstrate freedom of navigation, the United States sent ships of the Sixth Fleet into the Mediterranean with orders to cross the "line of death." When Libya fired antiaircraft missile at planes operating from American carriers, the United States responded by making several attacks on Libyan ships, sinking two of them, and bombing a SAM launching site in Libya. The United States withdrew from the Gulf of Sidra after five days.

A-7 Corsairs, operating from the carriers *Coral Sea*, *Saratoga* and *America*, played a key role in the conflict. In its air attacks on enemy targets, the Navy demonstrated it had learned to use electronics to evade missiles fired at Navy planes and ships.

Before the A-7s took to the air, EA-6B Prowler electronics planes picked up frequencies being used by Libyan radar sites. This information was radioed back to the carriers and given to weapons officers who were to fly A-7 Corsair attack aircraft.

These aircraft were armed with HARM, a high-speed antiradiation missile. It is an air-to-surface missile that is designed to destroy, or at least subdue, enemy air defense systems. It performs its job by homing in on the radar signals given off by enemy surface-to-air missiles and radar-directed antiaircraft guns.

Its wings folded, an A-7 awaits the call to action aboard the carrier America. (George Sullivan)

HARM, which replaced the Shrike and Standard Arm missiles in the Navy's arsenal, is 13 feet in length, 9½ inches in diameter and weighs close to 800 pounds. It supports a 150-pound warhead.

Comparing it to the missiles it replaced, one Navy officer said, "HARM covers a large frequency band of enemy radar and is a very high speed weapon. In addition, it has a much longer range and leaves a much larger footprint."

When the Corsairs were 10 to 12 miles from the town of Sidra, they launched their attack. The HARM missiles locked onto the Libyan radar signals and followed them at supersonic speeds to the ground.

If the Libyan radar operators tried changing frequencies while a HARM was on its way, the missile's sensors picked them up. The missile's computer then ordered the missile's radar to switch to the new frequency. With their radar gone, the Libyans could no longer fire missiles of their own.

A-6 Intruders attacked Libyan naval vessels, which were small in size when compared to U.S. destroyers or cruisers, with Harpoon missiles. Launched from low levels, the Harpoon skims across the water's surface like a torpedo, then suddenly pitches up into the air to dive on its target.

The radar-guided Harpoon is 12½ feet in length, 13 inches in diameter and weighs 1,100 pounds. It carries a 570-pound warhead, which it can put on a target more than 600 miles away.

After the Intruders fired their Harpoons, they sped closer to the target to drop Rockeye cluster bombs, each of which is loaded with 274 small warheads. It is believed the Rockeyes sunk a small, fast Libyan naval vessel in the Gulf of Sidra. The ship was armed with surface-to-air and surface-to-surface missiles.

After the U.S. Navy had completed its operation in the Gulf of Sidra, President Reagan said the Sixth Fleet had upheld "the fundamental principle of freedom of the seas." The operation marked the 19th time the United States had conducted naval operations in the area since 1981.

The A-7 was back in action again during the war in the Persian Gulf. Two squadrons of Corsairs from the carrier *John F. Kennedy* were involved in virtually every major air strike of the war.

Said Commander John Leenhouts, second in command of one of the squadrons: "We were the only aircraft in the Navy's inventory that could haul the 'mail' regularly with a high probability of survival over the distances involved."

"A couple of times we traveled over 1,400 miles round trip—about a five-hour mission," said another officer. "Not too many aircraft can do that as consistently as the A-7."

Besides their importance as strike planes in the Persian Gulf, Navy aircraft also played a vital role in gaining control of the electronic battlefield. Before each air strike, Navy EA-6B Prowlers and Air Force EF-111 Ravens, loaded with powerful jamming gear, cleared the way.

When Commander Leenhouts guided his A-7 Corsair II through the night sky toward Baghdad, tiny blips on his radar screen indicated the approach of Soviet built MiGs. He got ready for a fight. Then, before the first missile was fired, it was over. "They acted as if they were overwhelmed," said Commander Leenhouts. "In such cases, I don't think they had a very clear picture of what was out there."

Commander Leenhouts was right. What had happened was that the jammers had cut off the enemy planes from their control center. They had no choice but to flee. "When you knock out their eyes from the ground, these guys are blind," said one Air Force colonel.

During Operation Desert Storm, the two squadrons of A-7s from the *Kennedy* delivered more than 2 million pounds of bombs and missiles while flying 745 combat missions. They won high praise for their dependability. Captain Phil Gay, commanding officer of the *Kennedy*,

An A-7 is catapulted into the air while another prepares for launch, during air operations aboard the carrier Nimitz. (George Sullivan)

said the A-7 squadrons had the "best maintenance record of any two squadrons I've ever seen." He added: "They tended to have almost all of their aircraft up every day. On two occasions they had 19 A-7s flying on missions. That's amazing, considering we had only 20 on the ship and one was broke."

Operation Desert Storm marked the last time the A-7 would see action. The Navy had been replacing the plane with the F/A-18 Hornet, a strike fighter. When the *John F. Kennedy* returned to its home port from the Persian Gulf, its A-7s were removed in favor of F/A-18s.

The A-7 carried on a tradition of notable Navy attack planes, begun during World War II with the SBD Dauntless and F-4U Corsair, and continued by the A-1 Skyraider and A-4 Skyhawk. "It's stood the test of time and proven the technology of the '60s was a quality product," said Commander Leenhouts. "It's a testament to the people who push it, drive it, fix it, and make it work." He called it "another great" in naval aviation.

10   TUPOLEV Tu-95/142 BEAR

In the decades before the Soviet Union broke apart, decades in which that nation was often engaged in Cold War competition with the United States and its North Atlantic Treaty Organization allies, Soviet policy was never to discard any equipment that still might find a use, despite the development of superior types. Tu-95/142 Bear was evidence of that policy.

A remarkable propeller-driven aircraft, the Bear was an important weapon in the Soviet Union right up until 1991. The U.S. Air Force once described the Bear as "a formidable spearhead of Soviet strategic nuclear attack and maritime air power." And the Department of Defense, in its publication *Soviet Military Power*, warned that the Bear, along with the Tu-160 Blackjack, gave the Soviet Union the ability to attack the United States with hundreds of difficult-to-detect, long-range, low-flying cruise missiles.

When the Department of Defense and U.S. Air Force made these evaluations, perhaps they had in mind those Bears that had been deployed at air bases in Cuba and were often encountered in airspace over the eastern United States. Or perhaps they were thinking of those Bears based in the south-central Soviet Union that used to carry out training missions over the United States and Canada.

There were also missile-armed Bears, perhaps operating out of Cam Ranh Bay in Vietnam, that once flew regular training missions against land and naval targets in the northern Pacific.

When the Tu-95 Bear went into service in 1956, the aircraft helped to make the Soviet Union a true global power. Almost any place on earth was within reach of the enormous plane and its massive load of weapons.

Through the years, the Bear underwent countless changes in design. Present-day models are so different from earlier versions that the

Despite its prop-driven engines, the Tu-95/142 Bear was important to the Soviet air force from the late 1950s until the breakup of the USSR in 1991. (National Air & Space Museum)

aircraft's designation was changed from Tu-95 for the original models to Tu-142 for aircraft built after 1968.

Different versions of the Bear included:

Bear-A—The original Tu-95 strategic bomber, first shown during Aviation Day maneuvers at Tushimo, near Moscow, in 1955, the Bear-A was capable of delivering either nuclear or conventional weapons. Its defensive armament consisted of three pairs of 23-mm cannons in manned turrets located on the back and in the belly and tail of the aircraft.

Bear-B—Similar to the Bear-A, the Bear-B had the ability to carry a large air-to-surface missile, designated the Kangaroo by NATO, beneath the fuselage. A few Bear-Bs operated as naval reconnaissance aircraft.

Tu-95/142 FACT SHEET

Designer: Tupolev OKB

Type: Long-range strategic bomber

Engines: Four Kuznetsov NK-12MV turboprops, each delivering 14,795 lb. of thrust

Crew: Normal crew of eight (in original version)—two pilots side by side, two radar operators/navigators, two engineer/gunners, one bombardier, one gunner

Length: 62 ft., 5 in.

Height: 39 ft., 9 in.

Wingspan: 167 ft., 8 in.

Loaded Weight: 414,470 lb.

Performance:

    Maximum Speed: 575 mph

    Service Ceiling: 44,300 ft.

    Range: 5,185 miles

First Flight: Fall 1954

Bear-C—Another strategic bomber, the Bear-C was also able to carry the Kangaroo air-to-surface missile. The aircraft was also fitted with additional electronic equipment for intelligence gathering. A refueling probe that jutted out from the nose was standard equipment on all Bear-Cs.

Bear-D—First seen in 1967, this was a naval reconnaissance version of the Tu-95 and carried no offensive weapons. Instead, it was equipped with additional radar and intelligence-gathering systems. One of the Bear-D's assignments was to pinpoint oceangoing targets for missile-launching crews on ships.

Bear-E—This was another reconnaissance version of the Tu-95. It featured several camera windows in the bomb bay doors. Only a few Bear-Es were built.

Bear-F—With a slightly longer fuselage, this was the first of the Bears to be designated a Tu-142. Used by the Soviet Naval Air Force, it served as an antisubmarine aircraft. It had two storage bays for torpedoes, nuclear depth charges and sonobuoys, which are anchored floats that use sonar to detect and locate submarines. One of the plane's storage bays replaced the usual belly gun turret. Some 65 Bear-Fs were on active duty in 1990.

Early in 1988, India took delivery of five Bear-Fs. Assigned to the Indian Navy and stationed at Goa, a base on the Indian Ocean about 250 miles south of Bombay, the planes are used for naval reconnaissance.

Bear-G—Another Tu-95, and similar to the Bear-B and Bear-C, this aircraft could carry two Kitchen supersonic air-to-surface missiles instead of merely one Kangaroo. It was also fitted with special equipment that enabled the plane to carry out intelligence-gathering missions. About 50 Bear-Gs were in service in 1990.

Bear-H—Based on the Tu-142 airframe, this aircraft was equipped to carry long-range cruise missiles, that is, long-range, low-flying guided missiles. The Bear-H has been in production since 1984.

Bear-J—First observed in 1986, this aircraft operated with the Soviet Union's Northern and Pacific fleets, serving as an aerial command post, an actual link between high-level commanders and nuclear submarines.

About 160 Bears flew with the Soviet Air Force. Most of these were missile-carrying Bear-Gs or Bear-Hs.

In the summer of 1990, after relations between the United States and the Soviet Union had thawed a good bit, the two nations agreed to show each other some of their heavy bombers. The purpose was to demonstrate features that distinguished bombers carrying long-range cruise missiles from those that do not.

The Bear often overflew units of the U.S. Navy. This mission attracted F-14 Tomcats. (National Air & Space Museum)

Soviet military experts were given a close-up look at two Air Force B-1B bombers at the Grand Forks Air Force Base in North Dakota. A U.S. team examined a Bear-G and Bear-H at Uzin/Chepelevka air base about 30 miles south of Kiev. The Americans remarked about the differences in the lengths of the two aircraft, the size of the bomb bays and the defensive armament the planes carried. What they had to say about those old prop engines was never recorded.

11 PANAVIA TORNADO IDS

"The world's most advanced strike aircraft."
"The most capable aircraft of its size ever built."
"The most important military aircraft in Western Europe."

That's how military experts have described the Tornado, a long-range, all-weather attack aircraft whose chief mission is to strike heavily defended surface targets. During the war in the Persian Gulf, Royal Air Force Tornados did just that. The plane was an airfield buster.

The Panavia Tornado is flown by the air forces of Great Britain, Germany and Italy. These represent Great Britain's Royal Air Force. (Panavis Aircraft)

The Tornado is an unusual airplane because it represents a cooperative effort by aeronautical companies representing three European nations. The aircraft had its beginnings in the early 1960s, when Great

PANAVIA TORNADO IDS

Manufacturer: Panavia Aircraft

Type: All-weather multipurpose combat aircraft

Engines: Two Turbo-Union RB 199-34 MK 101 turbofan
  engines, each delivering 18,000 pounds of thrust

Crew: Pilot and navigator

Length: 59 ft., 4 in.

Height: 18 ft., 8¼ in.

Wingspan:

  Fully Swept: 28 ft., 2½ in.

  Fully Spread: 45 ft., 7¼ in.

Loaded Weight: 61,700 lb.

Performance:

  Maximum Speed: 1,650 mph

  Service Ceiling: 60,000 ft.

  Range: 1,720 miles

First Flight: 1979

Britain's Royal Air Force began developing what was expected to be the most advanced tactical strike and reconnaissance aircraft in the world, the TSR-2. The aircraft was going to be capable of cruising at twice the speed of sound and beyond, while carrying a 2,000-pound bomb load. As a low-level strike aircraft, the plane would be able to sweep over its target at close to the speed of sound while carrying either conventional or nuclear weapons.

But rising costs doomed the TSR-2. The British parliament killed the project in 1965.

The Royal Air Force then thought about purchasing a number of American built F-111s to fill its need for a strike and reconnaissance aircraft. But the F-111 was having technical problems at the time, and increasing costs were a factor, too. The F-111s were never ordered.

The British then began to have conversations with several other European countries concerning the possibility of putting together a multirole aircraft, a plane that would be operational by 1975. They called the project MRA-75.

Germany and Italy joined Great Britain in the development of the aircraft, which was to become one of Europe's biggest industrial projects. A company was formed to design and build the new plane, drawing workers from the three participating nations. The company, with headquarters in Munich, Germany, was called Panavia.

The all-weather swept-wing combat aircraft was to play many roles, as specified by the three partners. The roles were:

- close-support/battlefield interdiction (Interdiction used to be strictly an artillery term. It referred to a concentration of fire on roads and lines of communication behind enemy lines for the purpose of disrupting movement or checking an advance. Now used by many air forces of the world, interdiction has much the same meaning.)
- interdiction/counter air strike
- air superiority
- interception/air defense
- naval strike
- reconnaissance

It was not intended, of course, that the new plane would play all these roles simultaneously. The aircraft was to be fitted with three underfuselage and four underwing attachment points. The weapons to be hung from the attachment points would be varied according to the plane's mission.

By August 1972, the design of the new aircraft had been completed. In the years that followed, nine pre-production models were built and tested—four in Great Britain, three in Germany and two in Italy. The first production model of the Tornado IDS (inderdiction strike) made its initial flight in Great Britain on July 10, 1979.

Just as Great Britain, Germany and Italy joined together to manufacture the Tornado, the three nations combined to train crew members to operate the plane. The Royal Air Force base at Cottesmore was designated as a training site. Fifty-three Tornados were supplied by the three nations for training purposes. Besides being schooled in how to fly the Tornado, trainees also received weapons and tactical instruction.

In 1979, the Royal Air Force began flying a special version of the Tornado, a long-range interceptor, a plane designed for air defense. It was intended to cover the Atlantic approaches to Great Britain, westward as far as Iceland, and eastward as far as the Baltic Sea. The plane would

The Tornado can race through the sky at speeds of up to 1,650 miles an hour. (British Aerospace)

boast a computer display that takes in the entire North Sea. The aircraft, first known as the Tornado ADV (for air defense variant), was designated the F-3 by the Royal Air Force.

While most of the airframe and aircraft systems used by the ADV are the same as those of the original IDS aircraft, some important changes were made. The front cockpit and fuselage were lengthened to make room for more radar equipment. A section was added behind the rear cockpit so the ADV would be able to carry two pairs of British Sky Flash missiles.

The Royal Air Force used the Tornado ADV to replace the BAC (British Aircraft Corporation) Lightning and McDonnell Douglas F-4 Phantoms. The Lightning, the fastest aircraft ever to serve with the RAF, had an outdated weapons system. Another drawback was the plane's limited "loiter time." It was a hit-and-run aircraft, unable to linger in the target area. The F-4 was also showing its age, especially when compared to such aircraft as the Grumman F-14 Tomcat and McDonnell Douglas F-15 Eagle.

Beginning in 1986, the first of 165 Tornado ADVs were assigned to Royal Air Force Squadrons. The aircraft was also ordered by Saudi Arabia to serve with the Royal Saudi Air Force and by the government of Oman for its air arm.

After the Royal Air Force, the German Air Force is the second largest user of the Tornado IDS. Germany ordered the plane with the idea of using it to replace the hundreds of Lockheed F-104 Starfighters then in service.

Four of the five German Tornado squadrons are based in the central and southern part of the nation. One air force squadron plus Tornados that have been assigned to the German Navy protect the northern stretches of the country. These aircraft are equipped with Kormoran, an antiship missile, carried on underwing and underfuselage pylons.

Camera pods hang from the wings of this RAF Tornado IDS (interdiction strike). (British Aerospace)

The German Air Force also flies the Tornado ECR, an electronic combat and reconnaissance version of the plane. It carries additional intelligence-gathering equipment, electronic sensors and antiradar missiles. The German Air Force has ordered 35 Tornado ECRs.

The Italian Air Force began flying the Tornado IDS in 1983. The first aircraft were based at Chedi. Italian Tornados are replacing Fiat-69s and F-104 Starfighters.

The first squadron of Royal Saudi Air Force Tornados to become operational were stationed at Dhahran Air Base. The squadron had formerly flown Northrop F-5 Tiger IIs. With the invasion of Kuwait by Iraq in 1990, the squadron shifted to the Taif Air Base to make room in Dhahran for U.S. Air Force F-15s and RAF Tornados. A second Royal Saudi Tornado IDS squadron was scheduled to become operational in 1991 or 1992.

During the war in the Persian Gulf, the United States supplied more troops and equipment than any other of the coalition nations. Great Britain ranked second. When it came to aircraft, the Royal Air Force furnished 42 Tornado strike planes, 18 Tornado air defense fighters, six Tornado reconnaissance aircraft, 12 Jaguar attack aircraft, 12 Buccaneer attack and reconnaissance aircraft, and a number of Nimrod patrol aircraft and Victor K2 tankers. The Royal Air Force, Royal Navy and British army also flew Chinook, Puma, Sea King and Lynx helicopters.

The Royal Air Force acted quickly once the government of Great Britain agreed to support Operation Desert Shield. At the time Iraq invaded Kuwait, a squadron of Tornado ADVs was stationed on Cyprus, an island in the eastern Mediterranean Sea just south of Turkey. These planes were on the scene in a matter of hours.

The Tornados from Cyprus and other RAF Tornados were given a very risky mission—the low-level bombing of Iraqi airfields. Flying at night over heavily defended areas, the daring British pilots had to skim low when making bombing runs, staying within a few dozen feet of the desert sands. "The margin for error is very small," said one British officer at the time. "Some of the American planes are a mile up. We are flying at 100 feet in the face of antiaircraft fire and darkness." He called it "the most hazardous task of the war."

Because flying close to the ground left little time for laying out a bombing run, much of the Tornado pilot's work had to be completed before his plane left the ground. For much of the mission, the Tornado flew on instructions from a small reel of computer tape inserted into a slot on the instrument panel just before takeoff. The tape contained everything from the flight plan to a rundown on Iraqi air defenses near the target.

As the plane went rocketing in for a strike, the pilot and navigator watched the computer screen anxiously. They wanted to make sure the disk had been programmed properly, and there were no Iraqi antiaircraft guns nearby.

Because Tornado missions were conducted where air defenses were especially strong, the air crew had to do their work in total radio silence, from the time of takeoff until they returned to friendly airspace. For squadron commanders, that meant an agonizing wait until each mission had ended and the crews could report they had returned safely.

The bombs carried by the Tornados had two warheads. The first blasted a hole in the concrete, the second widened and deepened the hole by exploding under the concrete.

The bomb package also contained some 200 small land mines. A timing device exploded the mines in the hours following the attack. The mines were meant to discourage work crews from repairing the runway.

The Iraqis reacted quickly to the attacks. After surveying the damage from helicopters, they sent out armored vehicles equipped with machine guns to blow up the mines. They used fast-setting concrete to fill in the craters and aluminum mats to cover them.

On the first night of the bombing, a British Tornado was lost when its crew reported an engine fire and ejected. On the second night, a Tornado operated by the Italian Air Force, which had assigned eight Tornados to the conflict, was shot down over Baghdad.

Within the first two weeks of the war, during which time Royal Air Force Tornados flew about 300 missions, six planes were lost. Four of them were flying low-level missions when they went down.

The Iraqi Air Force offered only the barest resistance to Operation Desert Shield. Once it became clear to the allies that their superiority in the air was not going to be challenged, the Tornado attacks on the airfields were halted.

Military experts agree that in all but the most unusual cases air power alone cannot defeat a ground enemy. The war in the Persian Gulf provided evidence to support that theory. Yet the single most significant aspect of the allied victory was the overwhelming air power superiority of United Nations forces. Great Britain's Royal Air Force, with its tough Tornados and other combat aircraft, made a major contribution toward helping to establish that superiority.

12   TUPOLEV Tu-160 BLACKJACK

Awesome. That's the word a long-time military observer used to describe the Soviet Union's swing-wing Tu-160 Blackjack, when the bomber was first sighted in 1981. Bigger than the Tu-22M Backfire, bigger than the Tu-95/142 Bear, the plane it was meant to replace, and some 20 percent bigger than the U.S. Air Force's B-1B, the Blackjack was a true intercontinental bomber, designed to strike an enemy nation in any corner of the globe.

Like the B-1B, the Blackjack was intended to carry its big weapons load through enemy defenses either at low altitude and high subsonic speed or at high altitude and at more than twice the speed of sound,

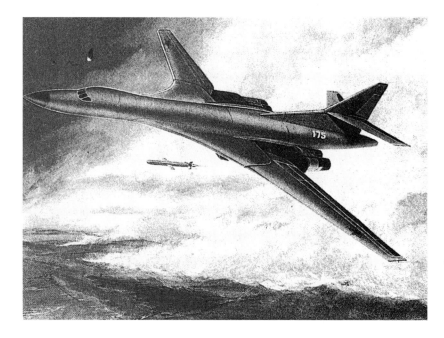

Published by the U.S. Department of Defense in 1985, this artist's drawing depicts a Blackjack launching a cruise missile.
(Department of Defense)

Tu-160 FACT SHEET

Designer: Tupolev OKB

Type: Four-engine strategic bomber

Engines: Four after-burning turbofans, designated Type R, each delivering 55,155 lb. of thrust

Crew: Two pilots side by side, systems engineer, navigator

Length: 177 ft.

Height: 42 ft.

Wingspan:

    Fully Spread: 182 ft., 9 in.

    Fully Swept: 110 ft.

Loaded Weight: 606,260 lb.

Performance:

    Maximum Speed: 680 mph

    Service Ceiling: 60,000 ft.

    Range: 5,150 miles

First Flight: 1981

---

probably at Mach 2.3. It's "swing" wings, which could be operated swept or spread, were what made the Blackjack so versatile.

The Blackjack had two large weapons bays within the plane. Each of these could carry six air-launched cruise missiles (ALCMs) or 12 short-range attack missiles (SRAMs).

In the cockpit, the Blackjack had a centrally mounted control stick, as does the B-1B. This was in contrast to the yoke used in commercial airlines and bombers. "The Soviets must have found that it was better to provide their Blackjack pilots with fighter-type controls, rather than bomber controls," one expert noted.

Each Blackjack pilot had four throttles mounted just to his left. The throttles had round, lollipop-type grips, rather than the molded grasps found on the B-1B.

The prototype for the huge plane, parked at a test site near Moscow, was first spotted by a reconnaissance satellite on November 25, 1981. Right away it was obvious that the aircraft was not a modification of some existing aircraft, but a brand new model, a "clean sheet of paper," as one designer put it.

Among the plane's most striking features was its towering dorsal fin to which the tail surfaces are mounted. The four engines are placed in pairs under the sleek wings, which have a much sharper sweep than the Tu-22M Backfire.

U.S. military experts once believed the Backfire was a standoff bomber. Standing off, which means never getting too close to one's target, but firing from afar, is a bombing tactic that was made possible with the introduction of weapons that have their own means of propulsion. The standoff distance was only a mile or two at first. Today, it can be 2,000 miles and even more. Since the primary weapon to be carried by the Blackjack was the Kent air-launched missile, which has a range of 1,850 miles, military analysts were certain the Blackjack was set to play a high-altitude standoff role.

Another artist's drawing from the Department of Defense, this shows the Blackjack cruising at high speed with wings fully swept. (Department of Defense)

Then early in August 1988, Frank Carlucci, a former U.S. Secretary of Defense, visited the Soviet Union and was invited to inspect a Tu-160 at the Kubinka air base near Moscow. He was told that the aircraft also carries short-range attack missiles. The purpose of these was to defend the aircraft along its low-level path to its target. Such a plane was not standing off; its mission was to attack with free-fall bombs or missiles.

Military experts now look upon the Tu-160 as a versatile bomber. It was designed both for low-level strikes and high-level standoff missions. There is not the slightest doubt the aircraft was crammed with the latest electronic sensors, receivers and jammers to support its dual roles.

The first squadron of 12 Blackjacks operated from Dolon air base in south-central Russia. (It was from Dolon that Soviet Bear-H bombers flew training missions over the North American continent.)

The Defense Department forecast that during the 1990s, the Tu-160 Blackjack would be turned out at the rate of about 30 planes a year, the same rate as for the Tu-22M Backfire. A Soviet plant in Kazan, about 500 miles east of Moscow, was where the plane was to be produced.

But considering the social and political turmoil that beset the Soviet Union in 1991, no one can predict the future of the former Soviet Union's Air Force, much less that of the Tu-160 Blackjack.

13 NORTHROP B-2 STEALTH

In 1936, Sir Robert Watson Watt, the Scottish physicist who is called "the father of radar," predicted that one day designers of bombers would try to make their aircraft as "invisible" to radar as possible. About a half a century later, Watt's prediction came to be fulfilled by what are called "stealth" planes. They seek to fly through enemy airspace without being detected.

Accomplishing this was no easy task. It meant designing an aircraft without any big flat surfaces, which easily reflect radar signals. Everything had to be smooth curves. It meant hiding protruding engines deep inside the aircraft and covering exterior surfaces with radar absorbent materials that soak up radar waves.

In recent years, American military aircraft manufacturers have succeeded in producing, not one, but two stealth aircraft. The first was the twin-engine F-117, a stealth fighter developed by the Lockheed Corporation. First flown in 1981, the F-117 saw combat during the invasion

The B-2 Stealth was designed without any flat, reflecting surfaces; it's all smooth curves. Engines are buried deep inside the wing. (U.S. Air Force)

B-2 FACT SHEET

Prime Contractor: Northrop Corporation

Type: Long range strategic bomber

Engines: Four General Electric F118-GE-100 turbofans, each delivering 19,000 lb. of thrust

Crew: Basic crew of two, with provision for third person

Length: 69 ft.

Height: 17 ft.

Wingspan: 172 ft.

Loaded Weight: 376,000 lb.

Performance:

    Maximum Speed: Subsonic

    Service Ceiling: 50,000 ft.

    Range: 4,250 to 7,500 miles

First Flight: 1989

of Panama in 1989 and again in the Persian Gulf in 1991, where its performance was highly praised.

Northrop's B-2 Stealth bomber came later. Its first flight took place in 1989. It was not available for service during the Persian Gulf war.

While both the B-2 and the F-117 are regarded as successful, neither aircraft is capable of completely escaping radar's notice. "We never contended that stealthy means invisible," General Lawrence Skantze, who directed the Stealth bomber project for the U.S. Air Force, once said. "It means difficult to detect—and more difficult to track."

One of the earliest examples of the use of stealth technology goes back to World War II. The German Navy introduced a device that permitted their submarines to remain submerged for long periods of time. Called a snorkel, it consisted of tubes that extended above the surface of the water through which the submarine could take in air and rid itself of exhaust gases.

When German scientists realized that Allied airplanes might be able to use radar to detect submarine snorkels, they changed their shape so the tubes presented fewer reflective surfaces. They also coated the snorkels with a radar-absorbing material, thought to be carbon mixed in a rubbery base. The coating soaked up radar signals, allowing only a very few to bounce back to the sub-hunting airplane. In effect, the submarine had slipped behind a curtain.

Although stealth technology was well known, aircraft designers showed little interest in using it to outwit enemy radar. Planes simply used raw speed and their maneuverability to avoid being intercepted by radar controlled fighters or missiles. Or they sought to frustrate enemy radar with electronic countermeasures, such as jammers.

A turning point came in 1973. In a surprise attack launched on October 6 that year, the Egyptian army crossed the Suez Canal to attack Israeli forces in the Sinai. Egypt's arsenal, supplied with arms and ammunition from the Soviet Union, included the SAM-6 surface-to-air missile, which boasted a radar system that guided the warhead to its target.

The Soviets assured the Egyptians that the Israelis did not know how to defend themselves against the SAM-6. And the Soviets were right. SAM-6s tore apart the Israeli Air Force. Some 40 F-4 Phantoms and A-4 Skyhawks, which had been supplied by the United States, were brought down by radar-guided missiles.

After that experience, the U.S. Air Force got very interested in stealth aircraft. In 1975, the Air Force asked Lockheed Corporation to design and develop a stealth fighter. Several models were produced, one of which became the F-117.

Sometime later, in 1981, the U.S. Air Force approached Northrop about developing a stealth bomber. Northrop was the right choice. The

In designing the B-2, its radar cross section—its RCS—was kept to a bare minimum. (U.S. Air Force)

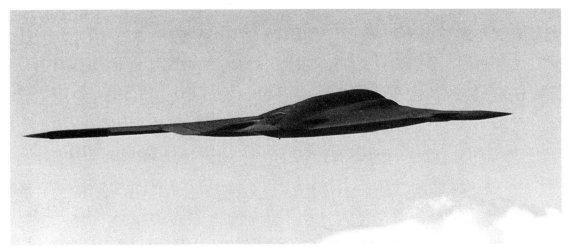

company's experience in stealth technology dated back more than half a century.

At the time, World War II was in its opening stages. The armies of Adolph Hitler were in control throughout Western Europe and England was under nightly air attack. For a time, it seemed the Germans might invade England and knock the British out of the war. If that happened, the United States would be left without any bomber bases in Europe.

Military planners sent out a call to American aircraft designers for a bombing plane that would be capable of carrying several tons of bombs from bases in the United States or Canada, dropping the bombs on European targets, and then returning to their North American bases. They wanted an aircraft that could carry a 10,000-pound payload 10,000 miles nonstop.

Of the four designs submitted, the most unusual came from the Northrop Corporation. It called for an airplane that was one pure supporting surface—no fuselage, no tail surfaces, and no exposed engines or engine housing. The aircraft was, essentially, a flying wing. It was designated the XB-35.

Two of the planes were ordered by the Army Air Force in November 1941. (The U.S. Air Force, separate from the Army, did not come into existence until after World War II.) They were to be four-engine aircraft. And the engines, mounted on the wing's back edge, were to have propellers that pushed rather than pulled.

Many problems had to be overcome in the development of the futuristic looking aircraft. As a result, the XB-35's first flight didn't take place until June 25, 1946. And it wasn't much of a flight, for the aircraft traveled only 3,000 feet.

But the "Flying Wing" did fly, and in so doing it demonstrated several advantages. It was an airplane in which every exposed portion contributed to lift, toward getting the plane aloft and keeping it there. Drag, the force that tends to reduce a plane's forward motion, was sharply reduced because there was no fuselage, no tail surfaces, no engine housings or other drag-producing surfaces. Increased speed and longer range were a direct result.

By this time, the Air Force had developed an interest in jet power, so a decision was made to replace the XB-35's prop engines with jets. The result, the YB-49, made its first flight on October 21, 1947.

In the years that followed, as flight testing continued, the YB-49 was often highly praised. After General Robert B. Ramey, commander of the Eighth Air Force, and one of the country's leading experts on heavy bombers, flew the plane the YB-49, he noted that it was the fastest

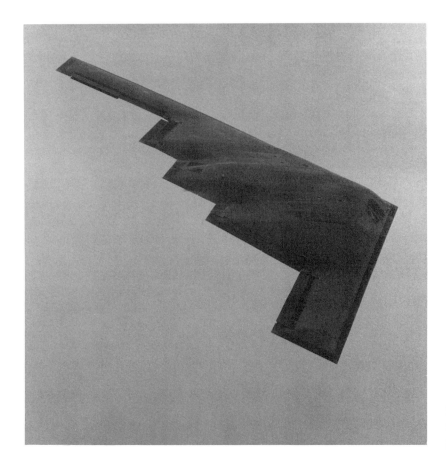

The B-2, from wing tip to wing tip, stretches 172 feet. (U.S. Air Force)

bomber he had ever flown. He described it as, " . . . a fine ship with a real future." The Air Force ordered 30 YB-49s.

One day in 1948, a YB-49 was returning from a test flight over the Pacific Ocean and approaching a radar station on the coast. The radar operators were puzzled because they never saw an image of the plane until it popped onto their screens while flying almost directly overhead. Since there was little interest in how aircraft and other weapons might be designed and built to evade radar signals, the incident was all but forgotten.

With jet engines, the Flying Wing could make a top speed of 500 miles an hour. But there was a big increase in the amount of fuel the plane required. And the weight of all that fuel cut the plane's range dramatically.

There were reasons to believe that under certain conditions the aircraft could not be controlled properly. One YB-49 crashed when its outer wing sections broke off during flight, killing all five crew members.

Edwards Air Force Base, the famous flight test center in the California desert, was named in honor of Captain Glen Edwards, who commanded the ill-fated flight.

Eventually the Air Force rejected Northrop's Flying Wing in favor of the B-36 Peacemaker, which, with 10 jet engines, was called "the mightiest plane ever built." All contracts to build the YB-49 were canceled. The Flying Wing stayed alive until 1953 when the Air Force ordered all existing planes to be scrapped.

Northrop's designers put the Flying Wing project in storage. Little was ever heard of it.

Then in 1981, the Air Force sought out Northrop to develop a sleep airplane with curving contours that would be able to escape radar's detection, a plane that the Air Force designated the Advanced Technology Bomber. Northrop immediately began dusting off Flying Wing plans and models.

Northrop created a huge computer network to help design the new plane. It permitted engineers to view every piece of the aircraft in three dimensions on computer screens. The drawings on the screens could be pulled apart; shapes and angles could be changed. The computers could test the strength of each part and report exactly how much wear each could take.

A B-2 Stealth takes a drink from an Air Force tanker. (U.S. Air Force)

The chief task designers faced was to reduce the new plane's chances of being spotted on radar, to make the plane "low observable." Radar works by radio waves that bounce off a target and back to a receiver that shows the target's location. Engineers designed the stealth bomber with

rounded surfaces to deflect the radar signals away from the radar receiver instead of back toward it.

They also built the plane so there would be fewer surfaces to reflect. The plane's four jet engines, the fuel tanks and weapons, instead of being hung on the wings, were put inside the aircraft. Air flows through ducts to the engines from small inlets on top of the wing.

The materials used were important, too. They included coatings of radar-absorbing material. RAM, as it is called, consists of carbon fiber, glass fiber and other composite plastics.

A transparent layer of gold coats the glass canopy over the cockpit. This serves to deflect radar signals that might be bounced off the pilots' helmets and objects in the cockpit.

What the B-2's shape and materials have done is reduce its radar cross section—its RCS—to the minimum. But designers were not able to eliminate it. It's an exaggeration to say that the B-2 is invisible to radar. If it gets close enough to a radar receiver, the B-2 can be seen.

And radar that is bounced from above or below would have a very good chance of picking up the plane, even at a good distance. Try this test: Hold a sheet of paper edgewise at eye level between yourself and a source of light. Now hold the paper at right angles to the floor and ceiling. The paper blocks the light, reflecting it back. Radar acts in somewhat the same way.

From the beginning the Stealth project was classified even higher than top secret. But most industry observers believed Northrop's aircraft would be some version of a flying wing. In the summer of 1985, Arizona Senator Barry Goldwater, chairman of the Senate Armed Services Committee, was shown a model of the plane. Goldwater confirmed the new aircraft had neither fuselage nor tail and its engines were buried inside the wing.

In April 1988, the Air Force released the first official picture of the B-2. It was only an artist's drawing and, as the Air Force admitted, some details had been "masked." But it was easy to see that the new aircraft was a flying wing.

That wing measured about 175 feet from one tip to the other. In comparison, the wingspan of the Boeing 747 jumbo jet, the nation's biggest commercial airliner, is 196 feet. The B-1B bomber has a wing-span of 127 feet. The B-2 weighs approximately 370,000 pounds, somewhat less than the B-1B at 477,000 pounds.

The trailing edge of the B-2's wing was a unique zigzag shape. Movable surfaces built into the wing's trailing edges served as the aircraft's flaps (controlling lift and drag), elevators (controlling up and down movement) and ailerons (controlling rolls and banks).

On July 17, 1989, after almost 10 years of development and a cost of around $22 billion, the batlike B-2 got off the ground for the first time. The scene was Edwards Air Force Base in the California desert, about 25 miles from Palmdale. Not long after daybreak, the strange looking aircraft roared down the runway, headed almost directly into the rising sun, and then made a slow ascent into the cloudless blue sky. Two Air Force F-16 fighters flew as escorts.

The two test pilots flew at relatively low speeds, never higher than 200 miles an hour, and reached an altitude of only 10,000 feet. The landing gear was kept down throughout the flight, as is standard practice during test flights. The plane was back on the ground within two hours.

The B-2 is flown by means of what is called a "fly-by-wire" system. A computer automatically and constantly adjusts the plane's controls. The pilot exercises his own control by sending instructions through the computer. The F-15 and F-16 fighters are among other planes that feature fly-by-wire controls.

During the early 1990s, the B-2 was to be flown to Whitemore Air Force Base in west-central Missouri, which has been planned as the main training base for the B-2 fleet. Whitemore was one of the three bases the Air Force designated for the B-2. All such bases are located near the center of the country, as far as possible from a missile attack by enemy submarines.

Hangars are to be built at Whitemore, each of which will be able to house two of the 30 B-2s that are expected to be stationed there. The planes will be parked in the hangars to protect them from sabotage.

While the Air Force admits it is costly to build hangars, they help to keep security costs down. Fewer guards are required and the planes can be better protected with sensors.

Keeping the aircraft in hangars will also help to protect against corrosion of the radar-absorbing materials that coat the plane. The planes are also better protected against fire.

The B-2 was in the midst of its testing and evaluation program when, on January 16, 1991, the war against Iraq, Operation Desert Storm, as it was called, began. Following President George Bush's address to the nation, Secretary of Defense Richard Cheney announced that hundreds of air strikes on missile and antiaircraft targets in Iraq and Kuwait had been launched to "destroy Saddam Hussein's offensive military capabilities."

Close-up of the B-2 Stealth during refueling shows cockpit's glass canopy, which is coated with a transparent layer of gold to deflect radar signals. (U.S. Air Force)

The war in the Persian Gulf served as a big boost for stealth technology. The star of the air campaign was a close relative of the B-2, the F-117A Stealth fighter. The F-117A had been tested in combat earlier. In the invasion of Panama in December 1989, F-117A pilots had flown two missions and missed their targets both times. So, few observers were prepared for the success the aircraft achieved in the Persian Gulf, where F-117s, according to the Air Force, hit more than 95 percent of their targets.

The F-117As carried precision bombs, often called "smart" bombs. They played a vital role in the Persian Gulf war.

Precision bombs were not used successfully until very recent times. They were first tried in Vietnam nearly two decades ago. But they routinely missed the targets at which they were aimed, even stationary targets.

The U.S. Air Force tried precision bombs again in 1986 when F-111 strike aircraft, flying from bases in England, were assigned to attack targets in Libya. Again they suffered a high failure rate.

By the early 1990s, however, the bombs had been equipped with a new generation of computers and new guidance systems. These improvements made for startling accuracy.

Any aircraft using laser-guided bombs is also equipped with forward looking infrared radar (FLIR), which is mounted in the nose of the plane. The heart of the FLIR system is a special camera with a sensing device that is kept chilled to 320° below zero. This incredibly low temperature enables the sensor to detect the faintest amount of infrared radiation given off by any warmer object, such as a tank engine or a cluster of humans.

FLIR converts the infrared signal into a visual image that is displayed on a computer console in the plane's cockpit. The pilot lines up the target on a cross-hair sight that is a part of the visual display. FLIR also contains a laser "designation" that is linked to the cross-hair sight. To send a 2,000-pound bomb plunging through the ventilation shaft of a storage bunker, the pilot heads his airplane in the right direction, gets the target in the FLIR crosshairs, then orders the laser designator to lock on to the target.

When the bomb is released, stubby wings unfold in the tail area. These permit the bomb to be guided in response to commands from the computer.

Beginning in the 1990s, critics started to question the role of the B-2, each of which carried an $865 million price tag. (U.S. Air Force)

The pilot can send the bomb on its way while in level flight, in a dive, or even when climbing. During the war in the Persian Gulf, an F-111 returning from a mission encountered an Iraqi helicopter in flight. The

F-111, having no guns or missiles, attacked the helicopter with the only weapon it did have—a laser-guided bomb intended for use against ground targets. It flew like an arrow to its target, blowing the helicopter to bits.

"I would not have believed ten years ago that we could hit the targets we are routinely destroying today," one bomber pilot told the *New York Times*. "War has changed completely for better or worse. The side with the smartest gadgets will always win."

The B-2 Stealth, however, was not built to carry precision-guided bombs. It is not able to deliver smart bombs, as the F-117A did in the Persian Gulf war.

Nor is the B-2 an all-purpose bomber, a workhorse bomber like the B-52. The B-2 was developed with a very specific role in mind. In the event of war against the Soviet Union, the B-2 was to fly deep into Soviet territory and drop nuclear bombs on silos containing intercontinental ballistic missiles (ICBMs). It was also designed to strike underground command posts that sheltered top Soviet leaders. The B-2's secondary mission was to seek out and destroy mobile missile launchers, such as the Soviet SS-24s and SS-25s.

Critics of the aircraft say that the B-2's role could be handled much more cheaply by cruise missiles. These, too, are being built with radar-evading stealth characteristics. Dozens, even hundreds, of cruise missiles could be fired from the ground at the same targets the B-2 was meant to take out.

The B-2 has also been criticized because it is a relatively slow aircraft, unable to travel beyond supersonic speeds. And the B-2 has no after-burner. This is the device that sprays fuel directly on the exhaust of a jet engine. When the fuel burns, it gives the plane an extra burst of speed. Since the Korean War, jet pilots have considered the added thrust provided by an afterburner to be essential for success in air combat.

Besides its slowness, the B-2 is also handicapped by a lack of weapons. Since its wing is "clean," it has no pylons from which to hang guns, cannons or air-to-air missiles. The B-2 goes into battle naked.

"The B-2 crews will fly with all their eggs in the Stealth basket," one engineer told the *New York Times*. "Once the bad guys spot them, they won't stand a chance of outrunning the enemy fighters."

By the end of 1991, Northrop had built three B-2s. The Air Force had planned originally to acquire 132 B-2s, at a cost of $865 million apiece. But in April 1990 the Department of Defense cut the number to 75.

It is doubtful, however, whether those 75 planes will ever be built. When tensions between the United States and the Soviet Union eased during the late 1980s and early 1990s, and a closer relationship began to develop between the two countries, critics began to question whether there was a need for the B-2. The aircraft's primary mission of dropping nuclear bombs on the Soviet Union had become quite meaningless.

President George Bush favored the B-2. It was one of his two military priorities. The other was the antimissile defense system, popularly known as "Star Wars."

During the early 1990s, congressional critics of the B-2 were success- ful in blocking money for the purchase of new planes. Even President Bush's support was not enough to win funds for additional bombers.

AIRCRAFT DESIGNATION SYSTEM

Planes of the U.S. Air Force, Navy and Marine Corps are classified by a coded system of letters and numbers. The letters indicate the plane's mission; the numbers refer to the plane's model.

Here are the various mission symbols:

SYMBOL	MISSION
A	Attack
B	Bomber
C	Cargo/transport
E	Electronics
F	Fighter
K	Tanker
L	Liaison
O	Observation
P	Patrol
Q	Targeting and drone
R	Reconnaissance
S	Search and Rescue
T	Trainer
U	Utility
X	Research

Planes designated B-1 or B-52 are bombers. The "1" and "52" indicate the particular model.

Letters that follow the model number indicate a modification, such as B-1B.

Two other symbols are used to indicate aircraft type. They are:

H	Helicopter
V	VTOL (vertical takeoff and landing) or STOL (short takeoff and landing)

An additional letter is sometimes used before the other letters or numbers. This prefix indicates a special status the aircraft has. The prefix letters are:

LETTER	STATUS
G	Permanently grounded
J	Special test, temporary
N	Special test, permanent
X	Experimental
Y	Prototype
Z	In planning or development

GLOSSARY

afterburner A device in the engine of a jet airplane that provides for extra thrust by burning additional fuel in the hot exhaust gases.

aileron A movable surface, usually located on the trailing edge of the wings, that controls an airplane's banks and rolls.

avionics Aeronautical electronics.

bogie Slang term for an enemy aircraft.

bolter A carrier landing attempt in which the plane's hook fails to engage an arresting cable, causing the plane to make another attempt.

burner Short for afterburner (see above).

carpet bombing To drop bombs over a large area rather than pinpoint a specific target.

cell A formation of aircraft.

chaff Metal foil dropped by airplanes to confuse enemy radar.

cruise missile A low-flying long-range guided missile that can be launched from air, sea or land.

delta wing An airplane wing that is triangular in shape. The trailing edge of the wing is the base of the triangle.

dorsal The part of an aircraft corresponding to the human back; the top of the fuselage.

elevator A movable surface, usually attached to the horizontal stabilizer of an aircraft, used to produce up and down movement.

flak Antiaircraft fire.

flap A movable surface, usually located on the trailing edge of the wing, used to increase an airplane's lift or drag.

fur ball the frantic tangle of an air-to-air dogfight.

G A unit of force equal to the gravity exerted on a body at rest. At one G, a 200-pound man weighs 200 pounds; at four Gs, he weighs 800 pounds. In airplanes, G forces develop in rapid turns, climbs and dives.

golden BB   Slang for unlucky shot from the ground that strikes a pilot or his aircraft.

incendiary bomb   A bomb that ignites upon bursting.

intercept   The ability to detect and destroy enemy aircraft.

interceptor   A fast-climbing, highly maneuverable fighter plane designed to intercept enemy aircraft.

interdict   To seek to cut or destroy enemy lines of communication and supply.

lock on   Slang term meaning to fix a weapon on a target by electronic means.

Mach   A number used to describe the speed of planes flying near or above the speed of sound. At Mach 1, a plane is traveling at the speed of sound. (At 40,000 feet, sound normally travels at 660 miles an hour.) At Mach 2, a plane is traveling at twice the speed of sound (about 1,320 miles an hour). The term is named for Ernest Mach, an Austrian physicist who died in 1916.

mort themselves out   Pilot slang for planes shooting one another accidentally.

napalm   Thickened gasoline or other highly flammable substance used to create incendiary bombs.

ordnance   Military weapons, especially heavy guns and ammunition

prototype   The pre-production model of an aircraft.

pylon   A curved or angular piece of metal that is used to hold or suspend various types of bombs, missiles or fuel pods from an aircraft's wings or fuselage.

radome   The dome-shaped housing for a radar antenna.

range   The maximum distance an airplane can travel.

reconnaissance   An aerial exploration of an area to gather military information.

Scud   Surface-to-surface ballistic missile built in the Soviet Union and supplied to Iraq.

smart bomb   A bomb with control surfaces, including wings and fins, and an electronic guidance system to direct it to its target.

sonic   Pertaining to sound.

sortie   The flight of an aircraft on a combat mission.

stealth   A technology that is a combination of design and materials that absorb and reflect radar signals so as to reduce the radar cross section of an airplane.

subsonic   A speed less than the speed of sound.

supersonic   A speed greater than the speed of sound.

thrust   The forward force created in a jet engine as a reaction to the rearward ejection of fuel gases at high velocities.

Tomahawk   An unmanned, rocket-launched, jet-propelled cruise missile fired from ships or submarines.

trap   Arrested aircraft carrier landing.

vector   The direction followed by an airplane.

wingman   Pilot of the second plane in a two-aircraft formation.

ABBREVIATIONS AND ACRONYMS

AAA Antiaircraft Artillery

ADV Air Defense Variant (of the Panavia Tornado)

AGM Air-to-Ground Missile

AIM Air Intercept Missile

ALCM Air-Launched Cruise Missile

AMRAAM Advanced Medium-Range Air-to-Air Missile

ARM Anti-Radiation Missile; an air-to-surface missile designed to home in on the radiation emitted by radar transmitters

ASM Air-to-Surface Missile

ASRAAM Advanced Short-Range Air-to-Air Missile

ATB Advanced Technology Bomber

AWACS Airborne Warning and Control System

BAC British Aircraft Corporation

BVR Beyond Visual Range

CBU Cluster Bomb Unit

CO Commanding Officer

ECM Electronic Countermeasures

ECR Electronic Combat and Reconnaissance (aircraft)

ELINT Electronic Intelligence

EW Electronic Warfare

EWO Electronic Warfare Officer

FAE Fuel Air Explosives

FLIR Forward Looking Infrared Radar

FMC Fully Mission Capable

FROG   Free Rocket Over Ground

GBU   Guided Bomb Unit

GSE   Ground Support Equipment

HARM   High-speed Anti-Radiation Missile

HAWK   Homing All the Way Killer; standard U.S. medium-range surface-to-air missile system

ICBM   Intercontinental Ballistic Missile

IDS   Interdiction Strike (aircraft)

IR   Infrared

JAWS   Joint Attack Weapons System

MRA   Multirole Aircraft

NASA   National Aeronautics and Space Administration

NATO   North Atlantic Treaty Organization

PGM   Precision-Guided Munitions; also called "smart bombs"

RAF   Royal Air Force, the military air arm of the United Kingdom

RAM   Radar Absorbing Material

RCAF   Royal Canadian Air Force

RPV   Remotely Piloted Vehicle

SAC   Strategic Air Command

SALT   Strategic Arms Limitations Talks

SAM   Surface-to-Air Missile

SLAM   Standoff Land Attack Missile

SMCS   Structural Mode Control System

SRAM   Short-Range Attack Missile

STRC   Strategic Training Range Complex

TAC   Tactical Air Command

TALD   Tactical Air-Launched Decoy

TOW   Tube-launched, Optically traced, Wire-guided (missile)

TRAM   Target Recognition and Attack Multisensor

TSR   Tactical Strike Reconnaissance (aircraft)

USAF   United States Air Force

USAFE   United States Air Force in Europe

WSO   Weapons Systems Operator

INDEX

Page numbers in **boldface** indicate extensive treatment of a topic. Page
numbers in *italic* indicate illustrations and captions.